CUYAHOGA VALLEY MICROADVENTURES

Revised Second Edition: ISBN 978-1-963588-12-5
First Edition: ISBN 978-1-963588-00-2
Library of Congress Control Number: 2024905061
cmvabook.com
@cmvabook on Instagram
Written by David Charlton
In collaboration with AJ Sekerak
Design by Emily Cordonnier
Cover by Sarah Schmitz
Colophon: Real Head Pro & Livory
Printed by StreamlineCLE

This book first appeared as a limited edition
of 220 copies, signed by David Charlton

DEDICATION

A society grows great when old men [and women] plant trees in whose shade they shall never sit. Greek Proverb

I'd never heard of Lancelot Jones before watching Ken Burns' *The National Parks: America's Best Idea.* The son of an enslaved person, bonefish guide to US Presidents, CEOs and celebrities and the first US citizen to sell his land (an archipelago) to the National Park Service—not the developers. Because of Lancelot Jones, America has today and in perpetuity, Biscayne National Park.

Burns also dialed me in on John Muir and President Teddy Roosevelt's famed Yosemite camping trip and its monumental role in the origin story of the National Parks. Those two happy campers—and ardent conservationists—had a bold vision, yes indeed.

But without a National Park Service to create, protect, and manage national parks in perpetuity, their vision would have been just a fever dream. And that's when Burns introduced Stephen Mather, who along with a huge assist from his right hand man, Horace Albright, showed up to architect and build the *bones* of our National Park Service. As the Mather Plaque reads: *There will never come an end to the good that he has done.*

I'm fairly certain Lancelot, John, Teddy, Stephen and Horace would qualify as good Ancestors—people who make decisions that prioritize the quality of life for the lives that will come after their own.

All of the above to share this with you: Muir and Roosevelt got me thinking about the visionaries behind Cuyahoga Valley National Park, John Seiberling (1918–2008) and Ralph Regula (1924–2017). And Mather, the boots on the ground making it happen, got me thinking about CVNP's third Park Superintendent, John Debo, Jr (1949—). To them this book is dedicated.

To John Seiberling and Ralph Regula, for your bold vision—seeing what we didn't even know we needed.

To John Debo, Jr for seeing it all through and more with sturdy and determined leadership.

And at the very same time...

Before Cooper was killed, I was grief illiterate. I have a wider aperture now—a deeper depth of field. And so, this book is equally dedicated to an often unacknowledged, if not forgotten, community of people.

To the families of the Cuyahoga Valley, forced to cede your lands and abandon your homes, farms, and a way of life lived for generations—your sacrifice heartbreaking, your grief ineffable.

I found myself drawn again to the Peninsula Library and Honoré Guilbeau Cooke's abstract *Mural of Transportation into the Valley*—a geographical pattern in pebbles of the Peninsula part of the Cuyahoga River Valley.

I no longer see the canal, the roads or B&O Railroad. Instead I see the homesteads, small businesses and multi-generational family farms Honoré would have seen in 1964 when she created her art. In the pattern representing the Cuyahoga River, I see an effigy mound, akin to the Serpent Mound in Peebles, Ohio. Dig a little deeper into the land and its historical landscape and another often unacknowledged, if not forgotten, community is unearthed: Indigenous Peoples.

At the same time as I see the beauty of John and Ralph's vision, I see the displaced families, their traumatic loss, and generational grief. I'm no longer dizzied by the disorienting dilemma of something being both heartwarming and heartbreaking in the same moment; we can hold both.

I can't help but feel it all as a real affection and warmth towards—and indebtedness to—those who came before us: the good Ancestors.

Mitákuye Oyás'iŋ

← *(Top) Honoré Guilbeau Cooke*
(Bottom) Mural of Transportation in the Valley
Photos Courtesy of Peninsula Library & Historical Society

CONTENTS

← *South Chagrin Reservation*
Nick Hoeller

PROLOGUE

Q: What do these five movies have in common?

1. *Jaws*
2. *The Godfather II*
3. *The Big Lebowski*
4. *The Lion King*
5. *Kill Bill*

A: Dramatic irony.

There are moments where the audience knows something the characters in the movie don't: like the mounting anxiety/horror for the hapless skinny-dipper in *Jaws*, seconds away from being a midnight snack for Bruce the shark. It's not my intention, however, to be dramatic or ironic or leave you wondering: *Did he write this before or after his son died?*

I wrote the lion's share of these stories when my partner, Susan, and I had three living sons, Cooper, Michael, and Maxwell. To honor those stories, bad quality writing and all, I've left them as they were written—like they were before Cooper was killed in a car accident in Vancouver, British Columbia on Saturday, May 7, 2022.

So yes, you'll read stories where you'll know something I didn't. And because the stories aren't chronologically organized, there will be some jumping around, back-n-forth in time, before and after Cooper died. I'm telling you this because you'll read microadventure stories where Cooper and grief show up.

This is a story for another time but if it weren't for Cooper, I wouldn't have finished this book, let alone published it. And if it weren't for Sarah Kerr the death doula, a microadventure story about floating a local river with Socrates to fish for Steelhead wouldn't be sharing the same page as one dad's experience being ambushed by grief.

Initially I thought Sarah (grief counselor, clergy for the unchurched) was bat-shit crazy when she drew a straight line from the years I'd spent microadventuring and writing to being better prepared to learn how to meet Cooper's death—to learn how to grieve. She pointed at the muscle I'd developed—a muscle (internal preparedness) for being able to go where I'd never gone before. I'd grown practiced at being an adult-beginner. I'd become conditioned to saying Yes to new things, scary things, even when I didn't know how I was going to do them.

Sarah also helped me see that all the years learning and exploring that fine line between the wilds and urban living had increased my capacity to be more grateful, resilient, capable—and curious. The new microadventures (initiations) had become invitational spaces to cross some sort of threshold into some deeper sense of who I was meant to be. The microadventures had created deeper connections to the land I call home. And Cooper's death had more firmly grounded my connection to life. Intertwined they increased my capacity for even more gratitude, resiliency, curiosity—and compassion.

As I did final edits on the stories from the early microadventuring years I saw they'd been marked by the hustle culture—a hurriedness to check the boxes as fast as I could on the CVNP bucket list of trails to hike (all 125+ miles of them). And I spotted the spiritually-dumb TV and grief-illiterate soul wandering around in those BCD (Before Cooper Died) stories, too.

As the years rolled by, bucket list events slowly transcended into more meaningful experiences as stoked and experienced anglers, hikers, bikers and surfers showed up to guide adult-beginner me into unfamiliar territory—enchanted places and spaces they hold sacred.

When Cooper died, Sarah showed up to guide me through more unfamiliar territory: sudden, unexpected and traumatic loss and grief—wild, feral grief. And the microadventures transcended further, into other realms.

Now, as I travel through nature on foot, on a mountain bike, in the packrafts fishing with Socrates or soar over it all in a sailplane, I see someone trying to take the medicine and practice the wisdom prescribed by philosopher and author Stephen Jenkinson:

Grief is the midwife of your capacity to be immensely grateful for being born.

And so I pray: My heart is broken. I never want it to heal.

David Charlton
Hudson, Ohio
Lake Erie Watershed
December, 2023

← *Cooper, Maxwell, and Michael, Northern Michigan*
Ann Charlton Adams

CUYAHOGA VALLEY MICROADVENTURE DEFINITION

Flying to Vancouver, British Columbia for a family vacation to hike, bike, surf, zip-line Sasquatch, bungee jump and boulder jump into rivers is an adventure. Biking 1,400 miles from Virginia to Florida is an adventure. A six-week mountaineering school in Colorado is an adventure. Driving to West Virginia on spring break to whitewater raft the New River is an adventure.

Mountain biking CVNP's Lamb Loop trail before work is a micro-adventure. Waking up on a Saturday morning and making a snap-decision to creek-walk Brandywine Creek to Brandywine Falls is a micro-adventure. Meeting up mid-week at noon with Team 4 to hike the Ritchie Ledges loop is a micro-adventure. Fishing AJ's parent's backyard pond after work and catching your first largemouth bass is a micro-adventure.

The term microadventure entered the outdoor adventure lexicon by way of British adventurer and author Alastair Humphreys. He defines a microadventure as *an adventure that is short, simple, local and cheap—yet still fun, exciting, challenging, refreshing and rewarding.*

The New York Times describes microadventures as *short, perspective-shifting bursts of travel closer to home, inspiring followers to pitch a tent in nearby woods, explore their city by moonlight, or hold a family slumber party in the backyard.*

I define Cuyahoga Valley Microadventures (CVMA) more broadly. For six years I've explored that fine line between the wilds and urban living. While the main

dishes served up in this book are my experiences discovering local outdoor adventures in Northern Ohio, each microadventure was paired with four more layers of local flavor:

1. The food we ate
2. The music we listened to
3. The people we met, and
4. The land and its historical landscape we learned about

In Creole and Cajun cooking, onions, bell peppers, and celery are called the *Holy Trinity*—and fat (butter) and flour become *The Roux*. Blend 'em all together and these five ordinary flavors are transformed into something extraordinary—the foundation for gumbo and étouffée (and an Atchafalaya Creole Omelette, topped with fried okra at Michael Bruno's Blue Door Cafe and Bakery).

In my big ol' goofy CVMA world, local food, music and people are the Holy Trinity; the local outdoor adventures and the land and its historical landscape The Roux. Blend 'em all together, steep for six years and my former life of ordinary routines became much less ordinary; outdoor adventures were no longer trapped inside the exclusive domain of vacations far from home. Yet the alchemy between Trinity and Roux didn't cool & collapse there; a transformation had taken place in me: a newfound *sense of place.*

In the world of wine, terroir is a concept that flavor is derived from a sense of place. Soil, microclimate, sunlight and water quality blend together to impart a distinctive flavor having characteristics of a particular place and time. For oysters, the same concept is merroir. Compare and appreciate the

difference between the merroir of a fresh shucked Fishers Island Oyster from Block Island Sound and a Moondancer from Maine's Damariscotta River.

More than just a sense of pride, the five layers of local flavor found in these Cuyahoga Valley Microadventures planted in me a deeply rooted sense of place—a soulful feeling of belonging that's more grounded than anything I've felt since moving here in 1970. Turns out for over fifty years, in addition to not seeing all the buried treasure hiding in plain sight, I never realized I was *just an animal looking for a home.*

How do I put into words this *sense of place*—the savory backbone of CVMA's Trinity and Roux—and this newfound love for my Northern Ohio home? On living and writing the outdoor life well, I'm still learning the craft—so I'm gonna cheat.

I've got a song that nearly perfectly expresses how I feel; a song that touches a chord within me and resonates with my head, heart, and spirit (the soul layer). The irony isn't lost on me that it's one of the songs that enticed a twenty-something me to run away to Rhode Island.

Whether covered by Shawn Colvin, The String Cheese Incident, The Lumineers or performed by the band who wrote it, Talking Heads, that song is "This Must Be the Place (Naive Melody)" [Live Stop Making Sense].

That's one of the great things about music. You can sing a song to 85,000 people and they'll sing it back for 85,000 different reasons. Dave Grohl (Warren).

← *Ohio Women on the Fly*
Jess Su?ak

INTRODUCTION

Unwittingly, this book got its start on a 2017 family vacation in Vancouver, British Columbia. And that family vacation got its start in a Lakota Sweat Lodge Ceremony led by a First Nations Elder known as *Old Hands*. Living and working in Vancouver, our host and oldest son, Cooper, was kicking things off on an adventurous note. My partner Susan and I had flown out to pile-on with Coop's two younger brothers Michael and Maxwell who were already in Vancouver. Michael was there wrapping up his gap year while Maxwell was preparing to start his.

While Coop curated the adventures (including a surf session at Cox Bay and catching a foggy sunset on Mackenzie Beach), he also dialed us in on the land and its historical landscape—and he introduced us to some colorful locals. Michael earned the nickname *restaurant whisperer* by mysteriously leading us to good, adventurous food each and every time. And like Robbie Robertson scoring a Martin Scorcese film, Maxwell intuitively curated playlists that accentuated the scenes and familial vibe inside that cozy Kia Soul.

These experiences, traveling through the days together, brought with them immense enjoyment, satisfaction, and meaning (aka happiness for short.) But then the hangover hit. When Susan and I got back to Ohio we returned to an empty nest, our grown boys having flown the coop. Some parents are happy campers when this milestone arrives; Susan and I were not.

To get the grief moving and chase the high from the family vacation, we decided to try hiking at home and flavor them like we did in Vancouver with local food, music and people while learning bits along the way about the land and its historical landscape.

In 2018, in lieu of jewelry, I gave Susan a homemade anniversary gift: a bucket-list book of CVNP trails to hike. Like our hiking shoes, we wore that bucket-list out fast. Over the next five years, as we met new people doing cool things in nature, our microadventures broadened well beyond hiking. And the territory we explored expanded, too—from CVNP to across the land originally known as the Connecticut Western Reserve (aka Northern Ohio).

But here's the challenge we ran into: some consider the 1988 opening of the Ohio & Erie Canal Towpath Trail to be the Park's most transformative project as it served as a mental map so CVNP visitors could finally exit their vehicles and explore the Park. Outside CVNP, however, no icon resource exists to explore microadventures across the rest of Northern Ohio.

I found it difficult to get a handle on it and tie it all together.

For someone who is not a writer, this became my purpose for writing this book—putting a mental map in your hands. My wish is the energy I've plugged into this project might serve to help someone in some way some day.

And finally, while this book may appear to be a generous map—forty-one microadventures, long lists of local restaurants, music, people and historical highlights—more buried treasure is out there hiding in plain sight.

← Gap Year Brothers, Cox Bay Beach, British Columbia

↑ *Like much of Banksy's temporary graffiti art, this expression of protest against eminent domain was short-lived; this Cuyahoga Valley home was torched by the local fire department for practice shortly after this photo was taken.*

(R) Erosion control on the Cuyahoga, circa 1974 →
Photos Courtesy of Peninsula Library & Historical Society

DYSFUNCTION, COCKY IGNORANCE AND A BOILING FROG

If you know, you know. I didn't know squat.

Since 1970, I've lived three miles from Cuyahoga Valley National Park (CVNP); as of 2017, I'd visited twice.

Once in 1974, the same year President Ford signed Cuyahoga Valley National Recreation Area into existence. On the way to get some sweet corn at Szalay's, my mom took my sister and me to Everett Covered Bridge to creek-walk Furnace Run. And once in 1979 when my high school friends and I hiked to a particular slot canyon for some after-hours shenanigans. And then with indifference, I ghosted CVNP for the next thirty-nine years. I blame dysfunction, *cocky ignorance* and a boiling frog.

Growing up next door to the Park, I was exposed to some dysfunctional behavior. While no-way-no-how would it qualify as childhood trauma, the experiences would leave lasting impressions I'd pass on to my sons.

Despite our not unique environmental issues (burning river, Superfund, etc), we'd somehow become the nation's poster child for pollution and dysfunctional ecosystems; a reputation that to a certain extent, we're still yoked to today, fifty-years later.

And while the CVNP vision was virtuous—stop urban sprawl, preserve historic and natural resources, agrarian infrastructure and the people living there—the approach the first Park Superintendent took in acquiring the lands of homesteaders, small businesses and multi-generational family farmers fostered fertile ground for conflict—and generational grief.

I wasn't against the Park; I was against the power and dysfunctional leadership style of Park Superintendent #1, Bill Birdsell. The general consensus was Birdsell's inconsistent and confrontational approach to land acquisition *thwarted congress, ignored the law of the land and overrode the rights of the individual*. People's homes and barns and buildings, which Birdsell called *visual pollution*, were torched and bulldozed—or as he called it, *obliterated*. By the time Birdsell was reassigned and the smoke had cleared, the destruction of communities like Everett and Boston was complete; an outcome which was never the intention of Congress's enabling legislation.

As a young boy, teenager and young adult, I saw the pollution, smelled the dead river, felt the anger rising from the valley and heard the constant yelling and screaming—and crying. Lasting impressions that began to solidify into something Mark Twain would call *cocky ignorance*. I grew to believe CVNP's 33,000 acres of pieces and parts would never measure up to the conviction of Pulitzer Prize-winning author Wallace Stegner that *National Parks are the best idea we've ever had*.

But in April of 1988, equipped with hard-knocks experience and knowledge gained at such diverse national park units as Acadia, Fire Island, Lowell, and Boston, John P. Debo, Jr. showed up to become CVNP's 3rd Park Superintendent.

Under John's sturdy & determined leadership over his twenty-one year tenure, not only did he execute on John Seiberling and Ralph Regula's bold restoration and preservation vision to turn 33,000 disparate acres into an honest-to-God National Park, Debo dialed in his own visionary adds:

- ☞ the transformative Towpath Trail and regionally impactful Cleveland-to-New Philadelphia Ohio & Erie Canal National Heritage Corridor,
- ☞ partnering with Western Reserve Historical Society's Siegfried Buerling to develop the Cuyahoga Valley Scenic Railroad,
- ☞ the acquisition of the shuttered Richfield Coliseum to prevent a shopping mall development catastrophe,
- ☞ the Countryside Initiative designed to breathe life into historic farmsteads in the Cuyahoga Valley,
- ☞ development of the Cuyahoga Valley Environmental Education Center, and
- ☞ initiating planning for the park's first mountain bike trail on the east rim of the Cuyahoga Valley, among numerous other hard-fought accomplishments.

But I didn't notice squat. During the productive Debo years, my *cocky ignorance* and I were in the bubble, working and raising three boys with Susan. And...restoration projects inch along very, very, verrry slooowly—and take a very, very, verrry looong time to blossom.

The *boiling frog syndrome* is an apt metaphor: it illustrates how small, hard-to-notice changes/threats in your environment can accumulate into big problems. In the case of CVNP, flip the script and you get how small, hard-to-notice changes/cool stuff in your environment can accumulate into buried treasures hiding in plain sight. Ribbit.

OTHER STUFF
Free on YouTube, the PBS Frontline documentary: *For the Good of All—the story of the making and unmaking of a national park in Ohio illustrates the difference between government intention and action.*

AT A GLANCE

BLUE DOOR CAFÉ & BAKERY
1070 State Rd, Cuyahoga Falls

**THE CATCH OF A LIFETIME—
MOMENTS OF FLYFISHING GLORY**
Peter Kaminsky

TRAPP FAMILY FARM
1019 W Streetsboro Rd, Peninsula

RG FOOT SPA
10071 Darrow Rd C, Twinsburg

OL'CHEFSKI'S BBQ
15 Trails End, Aurora

JIM'S OPEN KITCHEN TOO
9086 OH-14, Streetsboro

NEPALI KITCHEN RESTAURANT
399 E Cuyahoga Falls Ave, Akron

**WHOLLY FRIJOLES MEXICAN
STREET FOOD**
2404 State Rd, Cuyahoga Falls

**SEOUL GARDEN
KOREAN RESTAURANT**
2559 State Rd, Cuyahoga Falls

← *Pine Lane*
Gabe Leidy

In 2018, our very first hike (aka our very first microadventure) started with breakfast at Michael Bruno's Blue Door Café & Bakery. This place is busy and busy for a reason. I've had meals there *that I remember more fully than whole years of my life*. I stole that line from Peter Kaminsky's memorable book, *The Catch of a Lifetime—Moments of Fishing Glory.*

It was Smoked New Zealand King Salmon & the creamiest, most delicious, heavy-cream-finished scrambled eggs atop a toasted viennoiserie-style croissant (and a side order of bacon). Then Susan and I hiked Summit Metro Parks Overlook (Oxbow) and Chuckery trails (Signal Tree). From there we dipped into the Merriman Valley, past *The Portage* (Native American statue) and made our way along Riverview Road, following the Cuyahoga River north to hike the Stanford and Brandywine Gorge Loop trails. On the way home we stopped for some fresh eggs at Trapp Family Farm (Doc & Dan the plow horses), one of CVNP's Countryside Farms. Tracy Chapman, Boz Scaggs, and Caamp kept us company as we drove.

Winter, spring, summer, and fall, here's a short-list of trails Susan and I have hiked again and again and again—more often than not after a Blue Door breakfast (hint: Blue Door Bacon Sampler, Atchafalaya Creole Omelette, Lobster Ragout Biscuits and Gravy). These are trails with climbs, descents, some with creek crossings, waterfalls, overlooks, caves, river views, rock overhangs, and blowdowns.

Summit Metro Parks
☛ Thanks to *rewilding* in the Valley View Area, Celebration Trail (Don Drumm sculpture: *Sun Tracker*)
☛ FA Seiberling Fernwood Trail (suspension bridge)
☛ Hampton Hills Adam Run/Spring Hollow Trails via Top 'O World Trailhead

☛ Liberty Park Ledges Trail (nearby, treat your feet to a Reflexology session at RG Foot Spa and your belly to Ol'Chefski's BBQ)

CVNP
☛ Riding Run and Perkins Trails
☛ Plateau and Oak Hill Trails
☛ Salt Run Trail
☛ Ledges Trail via Happy Days Lodge/Haskell Run
☛ Pine Lane Trailhead: Valley Bridle & Buckeye Trails

Cleveland Metroparks Brecksville (Susan's Fave) and Bedford Reservations
☛ Hemlock Trail (plus Gorge Loop to Chippewa Creek)
☛ Deer Lick Cave & Bridle Trail Loop
☛ Sagamore Creek Loop (Linda Falls) and nearby Bedford Trail (Bridal Veil Falls)

Muddy Day Paved Trails
☛ CVNP: Out-n-back from Indigo Lake to Hale Farm (Bert & Eddie the oxen)
☛ Portage Park District: Trail Lake Park Loop (nearby, Jim's Open Kitchen Too and the Nature Conservancy's Herrick Fenn Nature Preserve)
☛ Summit Bike & Hike out-n-backs. Fave: 303 to Boston Mills Road (Boston Ledges)

OTHER STUFF
Like Waffle House, most of CVNP is open 24/7/365. Flip the script and after a Blue Door dinner, night-hike a CVNP trail on a full moon. Head on a swivel for CVNP's super-friendly Interpretive Ranger *Woody* Woodward: he has a unique story to tell. His Ancestors used to live on two Cuyahoga Valley farms.

CREEK-WALK BRANDYWINE FALLS

AT A GLANCE

SZALAY'S FARM & MARKET
4563 Riverview Rd, Peninsula

GREAT PLAINS
Ian Frazier

DAVE'S COSMIC SUBS
186 N Main St, Hudson

TINKERS CREEK TAVERN
14000 Tinkers Creek Rd, Walton Hills

SILENT SPRING
Rachel Carson

A GREEN SHROUDED MIRACLE: THE ADMINISTRATIVE HISTORY OF CUYAHOGA VALLEY NATURAL RECREATION AREA
Ron Cockrell (available at Peninsula Library)

← *Brandywine Falls*
Gabe Leidy

Furnace Run was my first creek-walk. While running an errand to score some sweet corn at Szalays, my mom took my sister, Annie, and me to Everett Covered Bridge—and we waded in. That was 1974, the year President Ford signed into existence the Cuyahoga Valley National Recreation Area. A year later a spring storm would wash away that bridge and I wouldn't creek-walk again for forty-six years—until AJ showed up in 2021.

AJ's microadventure involved creek-walking Brandywine Creek to Brandywine Falls—where he promised we'd experience a dopamine-rush as we stared up, not down, the sixty-five foot falls.

We hiked Stanford Trail to Brandywine Creek and waded in. Heading towards the falls, we scrambled up Shredder Falls, over and around boulders, through pools and over and under blowdowns. In his book, *Great Plains*, author Ian Fraiser (who grew up in Hudson) uses the Lakota word *Ichipasisi* to describe a route as *stitching* (crossing) back-n-forth up a creek; there's lots of Ichipasisi on this particular creek. As it had rained recently, AJ and I kept our heads on a swivel for flash floods.

Arriving at Brandywine Falls, AJ and I found that big left bank boulder resting a sensible distance from the cataract. We sat smiling, the pleasure chemical flooding our brains. Occasionally we glanced up at the tourists on the platform who seemed to be wondering *How the hell did they get down there?* Or *What fools.* Likely both.

We headed down-creek and picked up the Gorge Loop Trail and hiked it up and out to Summit Metro Parks Bike & Hike trail, past the Inn at Brandywine Falls, over the bridge, through the tunnel and across the parking lot to reconnect with the Gorge Loop Trail, then Stanford Trail and finally our vehicle. We road-tripped with the Black Keys to Hudson for a couple Dave's Cosmic Subs (extra Dave's Cosmic Sauce on the side).

OTHER STUFF

AJ likes taking a hammock on this creek-walk—you'll spot where to hang it (hint: it's near Shredder Falls). On the Gravel Bike Mitchell's Ice Cream Loop, double-down on the microadventure and lock your bikes to the guardrail at the bottom of Stanford Road; then creek-walk to one of the Brandywine Creek pools to cool off.

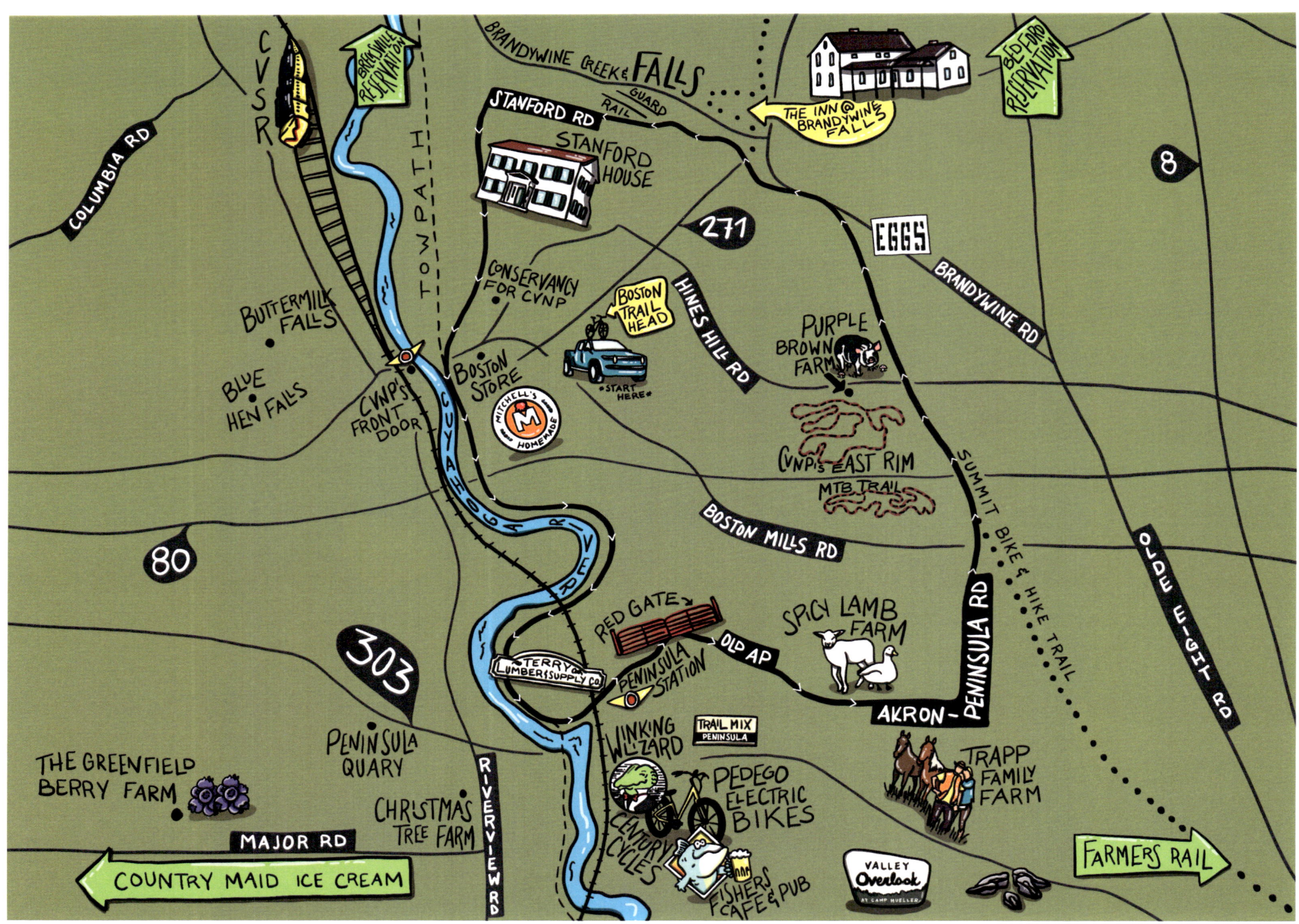

GRAVEL BIKE
MITCHELL'S ICE CREAM LOOP

AT A GLANCE

 CENTURY CYCLES
1621 Main St, Peninsula

 PEDEGO ELECTRIC BIKES
1503 Main St, Peninsula

 SPICY LAMB FARM
6560 Akron Peninsula Rd, Peninsula

 MITCHELL'S ICE CREAM
1550 Boston Mills Rd, Peninsula

 LUIGI'S PIZZA
105 N Main St, Akron

 DIRTY RIVER BICYCLE WORKS
110 N Main St, Akron

 ALL-AROUND CYCLERY
46 Ravenna St ste c-5, Hudson

 FALLS WHEELS & WRENCH
2445 State Rd, Cuyahoga Falls

 BLIMP CITY BIKE & HIKE
1675 Merriman Rd, Akron

 EDDY'S BIKE SHOP
3707 Darrow Rd, Stow

 BOOM'S PIZZA
14730 Detroit Ave, Lakewood

 BLAZING SADDLE CYCLE
7427 Detroit Ave, Cleveland

 JOY MACHINES BIKE SHOP
2605 Detroit Ave, Cleveland

← *Sarah Schmitz*

Gravel bikes are go-anywhere, adventure bikes. They rest between road bikes (skinny tires) and MTBs (fatter tires) and create endless opportunities for exploring Cuyahoga Valley and beyond.

This microadventure features mixed terrain: paved surfaces, abandoned roads, broken pavement, limestone and gravel. Gravel bikes with their knobby tires can navigate these conditions like a champ.

You'll bike a ten mile loop with two gut-buster climbs. But you're rewarded with a couple of long, fun downhills and ice cream at the finish. Or skip the gut-busters and rent an eBike (electric bike) from Century Cycles or Pedego in Peninsula.

Park at Boston Trailhead. Pedal the Towpath south towards Peninsula. You're riding to a red gate around the corner from Terry Lumber. There you will bike/walk the abandoned section of Akron-Peninsula Road (Old AP). This is gut-buster #1.

As you're catching your breath you'll be pedaling past a CVNP Countryside Farm: Spicy Lamb Farm (gourmet lamb & duck). Continue to Boston Mills Road to pick up Summit's Bike & Hike Trail. Just ahead is CVNP's East Rim MTB Trail System. Let your curiosity lead you to veer left, off the paved trail and ride the short distance to the MTB trailhead to take a peek at the riders queuing up to ride the loop. Once you cross the turnpike, just ahead is another CVNP MTB trail: Lamb Loop.

Enjoy the long downhill to Brandywine Falls to pick up abandoned Stanford Road. Bike/Walk gingerly downhill. Bike/Walk uphill for gut-buster #2. After catching your breath again, enjoy another fast, fun downhill. You'll pedal past Stanford House—and your vehicle, Mitchell's Ice Cream and CVNP's *front door* Visitor Center are just around the corner (check out the huge mural of the Cuyahoga Valley inside).

Some gravel bike resources: across from Luigi's Pizza, Dirty River Bicycle Works (Ryan *Otis* Adams dialed me into this microadventure). Brent Forrer's All-Around Cyclery in Hudson (Brent is an avid mountain biker and super-friendly dude quick to offer you a cold beer). Falls Wheels & Wrench. Merriman Valley's Blimp City. Eddy's and Marty's in Stow.

OTHER STUFF

At the bottom of Stanford Road, lock bikes to guardrail and cool off by creek-walking Brandywine Creek to Brandywine Falls. Or road trip Riverview Road north with some Black Keys, past Chef Ben Bebenroth's Spice Acres Farm (check out his Boom's Pizza) to Cleveland Metroparks Brecksville Reservation for a cool dip in one of Chippewa Creek's pools.

FISH FRESHWATER DRUM ON THE FLY

AT A GLANCE

 GREAT LAKES FLY FISHING
@greatlakesflyfishingllc

 GREAT LAKES DUDE PODCAST
Jeff Liskay

 OHIO WOMEN ON THE FLY
@ohiowomenonthefly

 CMNH TROUT CLUB
@cmnhtroutclub

 THE BACKPACKERS SHOP
@thebackpackersshop

 CLEVELAND BAGEL
4201 Detroit Ave, Cleveland

 LARDER DELI & BAKERY
1455 W 29th St, Cleveland

 KOJI ALCHEMY: REDISCOVERING THE MAGIC OF MOLD-BASED FERMENTATION
Rich Shih, Jeremy Umansky

 GREAT LAKES WATER WARS
Peter Annin

 THE DEATH AND LIFE OF THE GREAT LAKES
Dan Egan

 FLY FISHING THE INLAND OCEANS: AN ANGLER'S GUIDE TO FINDING AND CATCHING FISH IN THE GREAT LAKES
Jerry Darkes

← *Jeff Liskay and a Freshwater Drum on the fly*
Photo by unknown

Lake Erie—especially its southern shores and tributaries—is a world-class fly fishing destination. We know that doesn't sound quite right. One local angler and guide realized this years ago.

As a late July sunrise snuck up on the skyline, Cleveland's own *Steelhead Junkie*, Jeff Liskay, hauled Socrates and me out on dawn patrol aboard his Ranger to fly fish for Freshwater Drum.

Freshwater Drum might be Lake Erie's most under-appreciated, under-fished species to ever bend a fly rod. The drum Socrates caught (his first) put up a fight every bit as rowdy as its saltwater cousins, the Red Drum (Redfish) and Black Drum.

Freshwater Drum on the fly gets us close to the saltwater fly fishing experience—but right here on our unsalted home waters, our inland sea, Lake Erie. With gin-clear water and shallow flats to wade or paddle across, you can sight-fish myriad rocks, wrecks, and reefs. Jeff netted and gently released Socrates' Drum at a reef built from Cleveland's old Municipal Stadium. I caught and released my first drum at Cleveland Metroparks East 55th pier.

Yep, fly fishing presents a learning curve that requires dedication, but it comes with big self-achievement rewards and it's damn good for the soul. Not feelin' so fly? Jeff and Drum abideth by spinning rods, too.

Jeff owns Great Lakes Fly Fishing, is a Patagonia Fly Fishing Ambassador and pro-staffer for a number of companies, including Scientific Anglers and Scott Fly Rods. In addition to guiding, Jeff—one of the fishiest, friendliest dudes around—teaches fly fishing with Cleveland Metroparks, Ohio Women on the Fly, Cleveland Museum of Natural History (CMNH) Trout Club, and The Backpackers Shop. They're inclusive, inspirational, educational favorites. And Jeff hosts *The Great Lakes Dude Podcast. Presented by The Wet Fly Swing Podcast.*

Before we fished: Dan Herbst's and Geoff Hardman's Cleveland Bagel. Afterwards: Koji-cured pastrami perfection and oatmeal crème pie from Hingetown neighborhood's Larder Delicatessen. Larder Chefs/Owners Allie and Jeremy scored yet another James Beard Award nomination.

OTHER STUFF

Whiskey is for drinking, water is for fighting. Mark Twain. Speaking of water, our precious fresh water, Peter Annin's *Great Lakes Water Wars* and Dan Egan's *The Death and Life of the Great Lakes.*

RECONNOITER HELL HOLLOW

AT A GLANCE

 FAIRPORT HARBOR CREAMERY
202 High St, Fairport Harbor

 SCOOTER'S WORLD FAMOUS DAWG HOUSE
9600 Blackbrook Rd, Mentor

 MADSEN DONUTS
5426 Lake Rd E, Geneva

 EDDIE'S GRILL
5377 Lake Rd E, Geneva

 SOUTH RIVER VINEYARD
6062 S River Rd W, Geneva

 RED EAGLE DISTILLERY
6202 S River Rd W, Geneva

 STRONG CABIN
4888 Emerson Rd, Madison

 PARIS ROOM
7 N Franklin St, Chagrin Falls

← *Paine Creek Valley*
Gabe Leidy

We had our game plan: drive to Lake Metroparks Hell Hollow Wilderness Area and creek-walk as many waterfalls as we could find—not with the AllTrails app—but by winging it when the Wildcat Trail dead-ended at Paine Creek. If we got lost, we got lost—we wanted to give the hippocampus some exercise. A stranger had other plans.

As we hunched over a topo map at a Waffle House, we started chatting with a local who realized we'd never been to her neck of the woods—the Grand River Valley. She encouraged us to ditch our plans and go on a microadventure recon mission across Lake, Ashtabula, and Geauga counties—wingin' it on a grand scale.

We didn't exhaustively explore each spot, but when it was over, more microadventures had revealed themselves: hiking, biking, paddling, camping, fishing, stargazing and more. Here's the list of microadventures we microdosed that day:

1. Hiked Headlands Dunes Nature Preserve (Fairport Harbor Creamery—Boozy Milkshakes, Scooter's World Famous Dawg House)
2. Explored Lake Erie Bluffs (camping, birding)
3. Beach stroll at Geneva State Park (Madsen Donuts, Eddie's Grill)
4. Crossed the Grand River on the Harpersfield Covered Bridge
5. Reconned the *Church* Winery (South River Vineyard)
6. A wee bit of tasting at Red Eagle Distillery
7. Hiked trail at Hogback Ridge
8. Reconned Hogback Ridge MTB trail
9. Reconned Strong Cabin
10. Hiked trail at Hidden Valley Park
11. Hiked trail at Indian Point Park
12. Reconned Riverview Park
13. Brown bagged lunch at Paine Falls
14. Creek-walked one waterfall at Hell Hollow (shipload more)
15. Hiked Observatory Park (Certified International Dark Sky Park)
16. Hiked to suspension bridge at Girdled Road Reservation
17. Hiked Greenway Corridor to Chair Factory Falls
18. Hiked Chapin Forest Reservation (sunsets, nighttime snowshoeing & cross-country skiing)

Susan and I road-tripped with Caamp south on Chagrin River Road past Cleveland Metroparks North Chagrin Reservation (Buttermilk Falls), the Polo Field, Western Reserve Land Conservancy and South Chagrin Reservation (overflowing with waterfalls). We dined at a hidden Chagrin Falls gem—Sali McSherry's Paris Room (first time for escargot).

Whether you want to chalk it up to God, fate, the randomness of the universe, quantum entanglement, or the magic and mystery of Waffle House, there's something to be said for the kindness of strangers—and just wingin' it.

WHAT A DAY THAT WAS

The day began with the Grits Bowl at Waffle House—the clock on the wall said 5:30 am. Soon, under still starry skies, Socrates and I would be in waders and packrafts, paddling down a local river on dawn patrol, fishing for Steelhead.

On the drive to the put-in, I shared a story I'd just heard from Michael and Maxwell about their older brother, Cooper. When he and Mackenzie moved back to the Great Lakes region to marry and start a family, Coop was looking forward to fishing for his first Steelhead with Socrates and me; something we didn't know while he was alive. Socrates and Cooper had a deep connection to one another.

Socrates and I are happy as clams being on the water fishing together. I always feel a little sad for Socrates when I don't catch a fish as he's the happiest clam when I have one in the net—and vice versa (aka, *Compersion* Thanks, Micholo). Socrates is a gifted fresh and saltwater angler—and a patient teacher.

Socrates is an artist, too. Capt. Cooper Nash, a very cool and skilled local fishing guide, took us on a float trip where we both caught our very first Steelhead. Socrates walked into work the next day with a painting depicting the photo over there on the left. Every time I catch a new species of fish for the first time, Socrates paints a picture of it for me; no musky painting, yet.

On a skinny (shallow) river that Waffle House day, we portaged the packrafts 8,673 baby steps (4.1 miles). That supercharged the satisfaction when, on our own, without a guide and for the first time, we each caught and released a Steelhead: a blushing hen for Socrates and a chrome buck for me. Socrates caught two more that day.

Socrates can hold space for a grieving friend. He's never uttered fucked-up platitudes like *God needed another angel to tend to his garden* or a gem like *Mackenzie will be ok, she's young, she'll find a husband.*

Before we caught our Steelhead, a rogue wave of grief slammed into me. I can only hint at the ineffable as being ambushed: simultaneously cold-cocked, throat-punched, gut-punched, kicked in the balls, and table-topped. And it's useless to do anything but let grief's rip current take you out to sea: you can't fight water.

On the banks of the river where moments before we'd been quietly casting, I suddenly heaved over and flooded the space with *keening wails*—loud, super-charged expressions of wild, feral grief over the excruciating presence of Cooper's absence in my life. In this death-phobic, grief-illiterate, man-up, don't-worry-be-happy Western culture of ours, this death wail is some scary, disorienting shit to hear, to bear witness to.

Socrates didn't wander over and pat my back and say *It's gonna get better with time, Stay strong, Be positive.* He didn't say *Cooper wouldn't want you to be sad.* He just stopped fishing and silently and reverently held space until that grief-heavy wave moved through me. When I eventually stood up and locked eyes with him, I saw no fear, only compassion. For a guy who was born 200-years too late and calls himself a cavebear, it would take your breath away how eloquently he kept silent.

On the way home, I picked up some Bowl of Pho for Susan and Mabel's BBQ for me. After watching Michigan crush Penn State (Hail Yes; boom, Bunn!)

and taking a nap, Susan and I hiked the Ledges Trail and caught a sunset at the Overlook. Then headed home to shuck some Fishers Island Oysters.

On Sunday, Susan and I drove to Martha On the Fly in Tremont for a Betty, a Pearl and Karleen's Cornmeal Fries with extra Sunshine Sauce on the side. Then we headed to Mill Stream Run Reservation; Susan to hike and me to MTB the Royalview trail—a first for both.

I carried Ray Petro (Ray's Indoor MTB Park) in my thoughts until I rode through the pine grove on the Red Trail—and then it was all Coop. On the way home, we listened to Tyler Childers' "Follow You to Vergie" and Susan Tedeschi's cover of John Prine's "Angel from Montgomery" with her "Sugaree" coda. When we got home I watched the transcendant Bonnie Raitt and Alison Krauss duet of the same—and weeped some more: those fiddles get me everytime.

On Monday at work Socrates gave me a story he'd written about our Steelhead experience which included the blessing:

Adventures we never got to share in life we now share on this mystical journey of spiritual awakening for one and a renewal of faith for the other. Yeah, the Cavebear wrote that.

OTHER STUFF
That same Waffle House day at The Jake, while enjoying Momocho nachos and Fat Head's Sunshine Daydream IPA's, AJ and his dad watched the Guardian's extra-inning, comeback win over the Yankees.

← *First Steelhead and Socrates*
Captain Cooper Nash

TASTE THE TERROIR OF GRAND RIVER VALLEY

AT A GLANCE

 SOUTH RIVER VINEYARD
6062 S River Rd W, Geneva

 THE LAKEHOUSE INN
5653 Lake Rd E, Geneva

 THE LODGE AT GENEVA-ON-THE-LAKE
4888 N Broadway, Geneva-On-The-Lake

 STRONG CABIN
4888 Emerson Rd, Madison

 RED EAGLE DISTILLERY
6202 S River Rd W, Geneva

 IL RIONE
1303 W 65th St, Cleveland

← *Now, you're either on the bus or...*
Ken Kesey
Photo Courtesy of South River Winery

↓ *Stefan Gaspar*

Oregon's Willamette River Valley* is home to award-winning wines. Ohio's Grand River Valley has award-winning wines as well—and we can skip TSA lines.

Thanks to a microclimate with warm sunny days, cool nights and fertile earth wine grapes dig, our wines have a distinctive terroir. Terroir is the characteristic taste and flavor imparted to a wine by the environment in which its grapes are grown. In other words, a sense of place. (*Merroir* for oysters).

Established as an American Viticultural Area (AVA) in 1983, the heart of Ohio wine country is the Grand River Valley (GRV) in Lake, Geauga, and Ashtabula counties. The GVR has more than enough vines and wines for a weekend of wining and dining as well as hiking, fishing, paddling and relaxing at the beach.

Our son Michael, our friend Stefan and I kicked the tastings off at the *Church Winery* (South River Vineyard) and winged it from there. I served as the designated driver (DD) while they tasted award-winning Cabernet Francs, Merlots, Rieslings, Chardonnays, Pinot Grigios, Ice Wines (*nectar of the gods*) and more.

If you can rally yourself after a long day on the wine trail and your DD isn't too weary from driving your boozy bunch around, cap off the night stargazing under International Dark Skies at Geauga Park District's Observatory Park in nearby Montville.

And consider spending the night at winery lodgings, The Lakehouse Inn, The Lodge at Geneva-on-the-Lake or rustic lodging at Strong Cabin. Or pitch a tent at Geneva State Park or a Lake County campground.

OTHER STUFF

Cell reception is spotty. Before leaving home, download a map of GRV wineries and covered bridges. Hogback Ridge and Hidden Valley Parks have hiking trails with Grand River views and waterfalls. Atchison/Hogback Ridge North has a MTB trail. Add a gravel bike loop on the front-end of the GRV microadventure, then treat yourself to some Ohio-crafted spirits at the Red Eagle Distillery. You can pick up the gravel bike loop just around the corner—they'll let you park in their lot.

*Il Rione Pizzeria stocks former Cav's Channing Frye's & Kevin Love's Chosen Family Wines, located in Oregon's Willamette River Valley.

FLOAT THE RIVER

AT A GLANCE

 BLUE DOOR CAFÉ & BAKERY
1970 State Rd, Cuyahoga Falls

 SHERATON SUITES
1980 Front St, Cuyahoga Falls

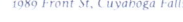 **FLURY'S CAFÉ**
2202 Front St, Cuyahoga Falls

 FRED'S DINER
930 Home Ave, Akron

 MISSING MOUNTAIN BREWERY
2811 Front St, Cuyahoga Falls

 SWENSONS
658 E Cuyahoga Falls Ave, Akron

 DEVITIS
560 E Tallmadge Ave, Akron

 BOULEVARD TAVERN
435 Chestnut Blvd, Cuyahoga Falls

 MOE'S TAVERN
1740 E 17th St, Cleveland

 THE FARMERS RAIL
98 Main Street, Hudson

 HIHO BREWERY
1707 Front St, Cuyahoga Falls

 OLD BROOKLYN MUSTARDS
4466 Broadview Rd, Cleveland

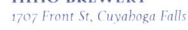 **MUSTARD MAN**
themustardman.net

 AKRON HONEY
21 Furnace St, Akron

 THE PIEROGI LADY
thepierogilady.com

 CLEVELAND KIMCHI
clevelandkitchen.com/kimchi

 PAV'S CREAMERY
2162 Front St, Cuyahoga Falls

 METROPOLIS POPCORN
2164 Front St, Cuyahoga Falls

We treated ourselves to a float down the Cuyahoga on a tube. We picked a nice hot day, grabbed our swimsuits and a cooler and lazy-upped for a couple of hours with Float the River (FTR). We leaned in hard by booking a room at the Sheraton and made a mini-vacation out of it.

When Savannah Snyder and TJ Mack—a pair of social entrepreneurs—started FTR, some folks scoffed at their Cuyahoga River-based, eco-tourism business model. Hell, some Internet troll posted FTR *would need tubes equipped with fire extinguishers.* IYKYK—like 20,000 happy campers who floated with FTR last summer.

After a jaw-dropping breakfast at Michael Bruno's Blue Door Cafe, we floated on FTR's Saturday 10:30 am trip. From there, we winged it for a long weekend in Cuyahoga Falls—a city that gets the outdoor recreation economy.

- Sheraton Suites (room with river view)
- Bike The Towpath, Summit Bike & Hike Trail, Freedom Trail, Portage Hike & Bike Trail
- Hike Cascade Valley, Gorge Metropark, FA Seiberling trails
- MTB at Summit Metro Parks Hampton Hills MTB Area
- Fish the Cuyahoga for Smallmouth, Pike, Catfish
- Ride the CVSR
- Rent kayaks from Burning River Adventures
- Buy kayaks from Falls Outdoor Company
- High Bridge Glens for a Cuyahoga River scenic overlook, across the street from Tiki Underground. You might see kayakers playing in the Upper Gorge whitewater. Don Howdyshell's Annual Cuyahoga Falls Fest. Don Drumm sculpture.

- **Breakfast:** Flury's Cafe (bodacious biscuits), Fred's Diner
- **Lunch:** Missing Mountain Brewery (*Prince Juice* & pretzels), Swensons, Devitis (Angelo's Hoagie)
- **Dinner:** Boulevard Tavern (deep-fried perch), Moe's, The Farmers Rail (T-F-R smash burger)
- **Beer:** HiHo Brewery (if the munchies kick in, HiHo makes killer pizza)
- **Night Hike:** If teetotalers with a flashlight, night hike the Glens Trail

OTHER STUFF

Before heading home, grab some fixin's from The Farmer's Rail. From their Brunty Farms to your fork, this butcher shop is a gem. While you're there, pick up some other local gems: Old Brooklyn Mustards, Mustard Man's Simply Horsey Sauce, Brent Wesley's Akron Honey, The Pierogi Lady pierogis, Cleveland Kimchi. Around the corner grab a 4-pak to-go from HiHo, a couple pints from Pav's Creamery and a two-gallon tin of Metropolis Popcorn.

CAMP CHRISTMAS TREE FARM

AT A GLANCE

INN AT BRANDYWINE FALLS
8230 Brandywine Rd, Northfield

FLOAT THE RIVER
2374 Front St, Cuyahoga Falls

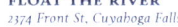
BURNING RIVER ADVENTURES
2025 Munroe Falls Ave, Cuyahoga Falls

HERITAGE FARM
6050 Riverview Rd, Peninsula

CENTURY CYCLES
1621 Main St, Peninsula

PEDEGO
1593 Main St, Peninsula

GREENFIELD BERRY FARM
2485 Major Rd, Peninsula

COUNTRY MAID ICE CREAM
3252 W Streetsboro Rd, Richfield

FISHER'S CAFÉ
1607 Main Street St, OH-303, Peninsula

APPALACHIAN OUTFITTERS
60 Kendall Park Rd Suite A, Peninsula

BACKPACKERS SHOP
@thebackpackersshop

FALLS OUTDOOR COMPANY
1727 Front St, Cuyahoga Falls

STAR WALK 2
Constelllation Star Finder App

MERLIN BIRD ID
Identify Birds you see & hear

INN GOOD TASTE
George Hoy

← *Dialing up the alpha waves*

Partners in life and business are ordinary miracles. Case in point: one-of-a-kind teams like George (1926–2018) and Katie Hoy who brought the Inn at Brandywine Falls to life, Savannah Snyder and JT Mack at Float The River, Michael and Gina Trebilcock at The Foundry and Moneen and Brad McBride at Burning River Adventures.

Carol and Kim Harimis are yet another CV dream team. They've built something special on their fifth generation family farm—a camping experience on CVNP's doorstep that feels private and adventurous—yet is short, simple and achievable. You can cowboy camp, pitch a tent or sleep in a shelter at their *Christmas Tree Farm* (Heritage Farms).

And your campsite is a springboard to more microadventures:

☛ Swim at Peninsula Quarry
☛ Paddle the Cuyahoga, ride the CVSR
☛ Bike the Towpath, ride the CVSR
☛ Creek-walk Brandywine Falls
☛ Hike Blue Hen and Buttermilk Falls
☛ Explore Ritchie Ledges, Indigo Lake, Everett Covered Bridge, Hale Farm
☛ Gravel bike the Mitchell's Ice Cream loop
☛ Mountain bike CVNP's East Rim and Lamb Loop MTB trails
☛ Mountain bike Summit Metro Parks Hampton Hills MTB Area
☛ Hail a rideshare to Blossom for a concert (Talking Heads with my sister Annie and Radiohead with Cooper)
☛ Climb at Kendall Cliffs climbing gym
☛ Rent eBikes at Century Cycles or Pedego
☛ Rent kayaks from Burning River Adventures
☛ Pick blueberries at Greenfield Berry Farm

Or do absolutely nothing. Putter about your campsite, read a book, or catnap under the pines. Build a campfire and cook some grub (or order from a meal delivery service). After sunset, night hike Tree Farm Trail or night bike the Towpath. Get a treat at Country Maid Ice Cream. Relax around the campfire with s'mores and nightcaps. Wake up on dawn patrol with the birds and bees and a cowboy breakfast—or hit Fisher's Cafe.

Arrive at Christmas Tree Farm in your vehicle. Or backpack, packraft, bikepack or bikeraft into camp. Or roll into Peninsula on the CVSR. Grab camping gear at Appalachian Outfitters, Backpackers Shop, Falls Outdoor Company.

OTHER STUFF

Star Walk 2 & Merlin apps. If you can find it, *Inn Good Taste* by George Hoy. A cookbook with delicious stories, too.

Nick Hoeller ➔

RIDE THE RAILS, BIKE THE TRAIL

AT A GLANCE

VALLEY CAFÉ
1212 Weathervane Ln, Akron

YOURS TRULY
8111 Rockside Rd, Valley View

DIRTY RIVER BICYCLE WORKS
110 N Main St, Akron

LUIGI'S PIZZA
105 N Main St, Akron

SZALAY'S FARM & MARKET
4563 Riverview Rd, Peninsula

SWEET MARY'S BAKERY
76 E Mill St, Akron

AKRON ART MUSEUM
1 S High St, Akron

MUSTARD SEED CAFÉ
867 W Market St, Akron

DIAMOND DELI
378 S Main St, Akron

NORTHSIDE SPEAKEASY
31 Furnace St, Akron

HIGH ST. HOP HOUSE
20 N High St, Akron

TOWPATH DISTILLERY
1824 Merriman Road, Akron

LOCK 15 BREWING COMPANY
21 W North St Suite TL, Akron

THE LOCKVIEW RESTAURANT
207 S Main St, Akron

← *Cuyahoga Valley Scenic Railroad*

Akron is basecamp for this overnight microadventure—an opportunity to bike that fine line between the wilds and urban living. In addition to your overnight bags, you need bikes, helmets, and Cuyahoga Valley Scenic Railroad (CVSR) tickets—purchase when you board (they appreciate cash versus credit card). CVSR staff will get your bikes on/off the train.

Starting at Akron's Northside Station you'll bike roughly twenty-five miles on The Towpath to Rockside Station—with stops at Merriman Valley's Valley Cafe for breakfast and at the end of the line Yours Truly for lunch. Then it's back the way you came, with bikes-aboard, riding the rails to finish where you started. Hint: stop into Dirty River Bicycle Works (across from Luigi's Pizza) to insure your bikes are up for the ride.

The 411 on this microadventure is intentionally lean—wing it. Just north of Beaver Marsh, pick up connector trail to Indigo Lake, Hale Farm (Bert & Eddie the oxen) and Everett Covered Bridge before rejoining The Towpath near Szalay's Farm. Lock bikes at CVNP's *Front Door* and hike an out-n-back to Blue Hen and Buttermilk Falls. South of Rockside Station, pick up Hemlock Creek Trail for an out-n-back that's challenging up, fast and flowy down.

Lots of options to choose from in Akron's Northside, Historic and Bowery Districts:

☛ **Hotels:** Tony Troppe's BLU-Tique, Courtyard by Marriott
☛ **Lunch:** Diamond Deli, Norma Touma's Sanabel Middle East Bakery
☛ **Drinks:** Dante Boccuzzi's Northside Speakeasy (secret entrance), High Street Hop House (Totally Baked Pizza)
☛ **Dinner:** Luigi's Pizza, The Lockview (gold fish), Lock 15 Brewery, Crave
☛ **Live music:** BLU Jazz+, Jilly's Music Room, Musica, Akron Civic Theater
☛ **Indie Movies:** Nightlight Cinema
☛ **Towpath History:** Richard Howe House
☛ **Baseball:** Akron RubberDucks
☛ **Enhancements:** Akron Coffee Roasters (ACR), Peanut Shoppe

OTHER STUFF

Last day, take an early morning ride: an out-n-back on the Towpath to Summit Metro Parks Summit Lake (a natural glacial kettle lake). Sweet Mary's Bakery for some pastries and ACR to-go and head to the Akron Art Museum and enjoy both in the Bud & Susie Rogers' Garden. Then shower, check out and for the finish, Highland Square's Mustard Seed Café for brunch.

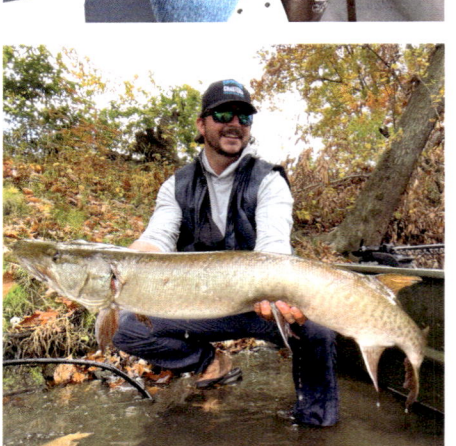

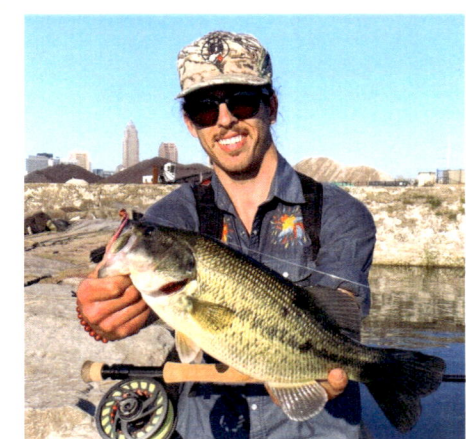

FISH YOUR HOME WATERS, INCLUDING THE CROOKED ONE

← (L to R)

Walleye, Jess Gantos

Perch, Elizabeth Durkalec

Musky, Jimmy Mucci

Biggie Smalls

Musky, Cooper Nash

Freshwater Drum, Jessica Suvak

Lake Run Smallmouth Bass, Jess Gantos

Steelhead, Socrates & Cooper Nash

Lake Run Smallmouth Bass,
Rainey & Jimmy Lampros

Lake Run Smallmouth Bass, Jess Gantos

Largemouth Bass, Jimmy Mucci

Night Moves, Jessica Suvak

These days, making a Cuyahoga River joke says more about the teller than the subject.

Socrates and I have paddled, floated and fished our packrafts down all five segments of the Cuyahoga River Water Trail. From the sleepy rural headwaters in the highlands of Geauga County to the mouth of the Cuyahoga at the historic Coast Guard Station on Whiskey Island. From mile 87.3 at the Kinsman Road put-in to mile 0 at Lake Erie (Merwins Wharf for the take-out at mile 1.3)

We've caught smallmouth bass (smallies), largemouth bass, rock bass, the under-appreciated freshwater drum, sunfish, catfish, carp, deep-fried yellow perch, and northern pike, the toothy ambush predator. And before we released them, we marveled at how each and every Cuyahoga River fish was vibrant, handsome* and stout. Along the way Socrates and I have seen mink, otters, muskrats and pissed-off beavers slapping their tails at us, deer wading across the river, herons, egrets and ospreys soaring overhead and eagles heading home with fresh caught fish in their talons.

One downside—since there's no yearly stocking program—the Cuyahoga doesn't see nearly the Steelhead (migratory rainbow trout) numbers our other tributaries enjoy. But times are changin'.

The Cuyahoga's deadbeat Gorge Dam is inching closer to being deconstructed. Water quality is higher than ever and keystone species are returning—bio-indicators like crayfish and freshwater mussels (ecosystem engineers). And restoration efforts are underway for Sturgeon. It wouldn't be out of the question to see a Steelhead stocking program begin someday. If that happens, the Crooked One has MVP potential.

OG MVP's. Over the past five years, of all the kinship groups I've been fortunate enough to learn microadventures from, hands down it's the angling community that has taught me the most. From super-friendly, super-stoked fly fishing guides Jeff Liskay, John Fabian, Captain Cooper Nash and Jimmy Mucci to super-friendly, super-stoked anglers Jessica Suvak, Jess Gantos, Jimmy Lampros, Aquatic Biologist Mike Durkalec, author/angler/guide Jerry Darkes, Jacob Jesionek, Wendell Mueller and Socrates.

Their multi-species knowledge and collective effervescence opened my eyes to our home waters teaming with world-class fisheries. In addition to the species listed above, Steelhead, walleye, giant lake-run smallies, white bass, bowfin, gar, and musky (the apex ambush predator) cruise our home waters, too. A diversity of fisheries that creates year-round fishing opportunities.

I feel an indebtedness to each of them as they've shared with me things they hold near and dear—things that in quieter moments, they might just say are held sacred.

OTHER STUFF
Volunteer for Cuyahoga River clean-up duty with Trash Fish and the annual Canalway RiverSweep. Hone your angling skills here at home, then hook up with local fishing guide and Patagonia Fly Fishing Ambassador Jeff Liskay for fly fishing adventures in Alaska, Belize, Chile, British Columbia, Labrador, Newfoundland, Ontario, and the Bahamas. Monte Burke's, *Lords of the Fly: Madness, Obsession, and the Hunt for the World Record Tarpon.*

*The pike Socrates caught was hauntingly beautiful.

Freshwater Drum, Jerry Darkes & Jessica Suvak

Steelhead, Jess Gantos

Steelhead, Jacob Jesionek

Perch, Mike Durkalec

Transcendent, Jessica Suvak

Freshwater Drum & Jeff Liskay by David Wilson

Largemouth Bass, Socrates

Lake Run Smallmouth Bass, Jimmy Mucci

Steelhead, AJ Sekerak

Steelhead, Wendell Mueller

Lake Run Smallmouth Bass, Jimmy Kompros

Sucker, Jess Gantos

Musky, John Fabian

Musky, Jessica Suvak & Jess Gantos

Tiller Time, John Fabian

Steelhead, Jess Gantos

Steelhead, Daryl Mummey

Steelhead, Jess Gantos

Northern Pike & John Fabian by David Wilson

Blushing Steelhead

Northern Pike, Jess Gantos

White Bass, Kim Koilpillai & Jess Gantos

Art & Sciences on the Fly, Jeff Liskay

Jessica Suvak →
Jess Suvak

PACKRAFT THE GRAND RIVER

GRAND RIVER

AT A GLANCE

SCOOTER'S WORLD FAMOUS DAWG HOUSE
9600 Blackbrook Rd, Mentor

FAIRPORT HARBOR CREAMERY
202 High St, Fairport Harbor

THE EMERALD MILE: THE EPIC STORY OF THE FASTEST RIDE IN HISTORY THROUGH THE HEART OF THE GRAND CANYON
Kevin Fedarko

GOODBYE TO A RIVER
John Graves

← *Anthony Smith bombs Plum Creek*
Anthony Smith

Thanks to Lake Metroparks, the Wild & Scenic Grand River—from Harpersfield Covered Bridge to Fairport Harbor—is damn near tailor-made for packrafting.

While you'll see plenty of kayaks on the Grand, Socrates and I appreciate the agility, stability and portability of a lightweight, inflatable packraft. It can be compressed to fit in a backpack—enabling you to hike in and out of remote areas where it's super challenging or impossible to schlep a kayak.

Packrafting is to rivers as a backpacking is to land. With paddle-in campsites at Riverview, Baker Road and Indian Point Parks, Lake Metroparks has you positioned for a paddling and camping-based microadventure—and a chance to packraft that fine line between the wilds and urban living. Keep your eyes peeled for eagles on the Grand.

What about pairing a packraft with a bike? Yep, you can bikeraft the Grand River. A packraft can be compressed to fit on your gravel bike, MTB or fat bike. And your bike can be broken down to fit on your packraft. Packraft + Bike = Bikerafting.

With a packraft and a bike, there's no need to drop a second car. After paddling the Grand, if you strap your packraft to your bike, you have a means to Atchison/Hogback Ridge North MTB trail, Grand River Valley wineries, waterfalls, the Red Eagle Distillery, the Red Eagle gravel bike loop, and your vehicle at Harpersfield Covered Bridge.

But maybe the idea of paddling the entire twenty-seven miles from Harpersfield Covered Bridge to Fairport Harbor seems too daunting; or you can't score a rez at the popular campsites; or you need to keep it short, simple and sweet. Dial it down with a half-day paddle. Socrates and I had a never-forget, woo-woo, metaphysical experience with a bald eagle while packrafting and fishing from Beaty Landing to Grand River Landing Park (Mitákuye Oyás'iŋ, Coop).

Before you head home, inhale some tacos in nearby Painesville or hot dogs at Scooter's World Famous Dawg House in Mentor (mountains of fries). Cruise Headlands Dunes State Nature Preserve (sandy beaches, dunes, lighthouse, beach glass). And swing by Fairport Harbor Creamery—you can't miss it—ginormous ice cream cone outside, boozy milkshakes inside.

OTHER STUFF

Paddle the Annual Grand River Canoe and Kayak Race (Madhatters). *The Emerald Mile: The Epic Story of the Fastest Ride in History Through the Heart of the Grand Canyon* by Kevin Fedarko.

AT A GLANCE

 RAY'S INDOOR MTB PARK
9801 Walford Ave, Cleveland

 MOMOCHO
1835 Fulton Rd, Cleveland

 RAY'S: THE INSPIRATIONAL TRUE STORY OF THE WORLD'S FIRST INDOOR MOUNTAIN BIKE PARK
Jonathan Allen

 CLEVELAND VELODROME
5033 Broadway Ave, Cleveland

 ROWLEY INN
1104 Rowley Ave, Cleveland

 LIES BETWEEN US
Podcast with Roger Bird and Ray Petro

← *Women's Weekend at Ray's*
Courtesy of Ray's

The 411 on this microadventure is intentionally slim pickens. Get to Ray's Indoor MTB Park and experience it for yourself—9801 Walford Ave, Cleveland. This is a story about a carpenter—Ray Petro. Context first.

Consider William Stinchcomb's vision for the Emerald Necklace (aka Cleveland Metroparks). FA Seiberling's vision for Summit Metroparks. John Seiberling and Ralph Regula's bold (audacious) vision for CVNP. Superintendent John Debo, Jr's execution of Seiberling and Regula's restoration and preservation vision with his own visionary adds like the Towpath, partnering with Siegfried Buerling on the CVSR, the Coliseum deal, the Countryside Farms Initiative, and funding the feasibility study that eventually became CVNP's East Rim Mountain Bike Trail. Imagine being so inspired to create something of such magnitude *for the benefit and enjoyment of the people.*

Ray Petro was—but not outside. Ray created something inside an old factory building. The boldness (audaciousness) of Ray's vision was to construct the world's first indoor MTB facility (200,000+ square feet). Petro's force of personality—along with his carpenter's toolbelt and loads of lumber—brought Ray's Indoor MTB Park to life for the benefit and enjoyment of every level of rider.

Ray epitomizes the best of northern Ohio—pride of place, an underdog with an indefatigable spirit, a builder, a creative, an entrepreneur, an irreverent, adventurous, blue-collar optimist with a grateful heart.

If you want to plug into the exhilaration of MTB, learn to ride inside at Ray's during the winter months. When spring has sprung—and trails are dry—you'll be prepped to MTB outside. Ray's is a magical space with a stoked, supportive community. And Ray's can rent you a bike—just bring your helmet.

A food truck is often parked on-site, but I'm hooked on Eric Williams' Momocho (for starters: smoked trout guacamole). Polish Boys and Girls at Real Smoq'ed BBQ. And starting in January through Fat Tuesday, Paczki's at Rudy's Strudel.

OTHER STUFF

Ray's: The Inspirational True Story of The World's First Indoor Mountain Bike Park by Jonathan Allen. Podcast: Lies Between Us—Roger Bird and Ray Petro. Check out Ohio's only velodrome complex—a cycling track with fifty-degree banked turns. Cleveland Velodrome's Learn-to-Ride class is free for adults. Rowley Inn and the Perogie Lady's pierogies for the finish.

SAIL LAKE ERIE

AT A GLANCE

▶ **UNTOLD: THE RACE OF THE CENTURY**

▶ **DEAD CALM**
Nicole Kidman and Sam Neill

📖 **THE PHONE BOX AT THE EDGE OF THE WORLD**
Laura Imai Messina

← *Lake Erie*
Meghan Winkler

By a show of hands, how many of you have been out on Lake Erie? On a surfboard, windsurfer, or kiteboard? On a kayak, sea kayak or SUP (Stand Up Paddleboard)? On guide Jeff Liskay's Ranger fishing boat angling for one of Lake Erie's Grand Slams: catching a walleye, smallmouth bass, and freshwater drum on the same day? What about a sailboat?

The last time on Lake Erie for me was on a freighter with AJ and Socrates sucking out contaminated water from the bilges of the SS Alpena (1942) for the environmental services day job. Before that Socrates and I were fishing at Cleveland Metroparks E. 55th Pier (Socrates caught a football-sized smallmouth bass and I a plump perch—which Socrates killed quickly and took home for dinner).

Let's tack back to sailing and talk about Michael and Gina Trebilcock giving our community the opportunity to learn how to sail Lake Erie. First, these partners in life and philanthropy established The Foundry *to transform the lives of Cleveland's youth through access to the sport of rowing at a world-class non-profit rowing facility.* Then they leaned in even further for our community by creating Foundry Sailing to provide access for all to a world-class sailing facility at the Historic Coast Guard Station on Whiskey Island.

Foundry Sailing offers comprehensive learn-to-sail programming. And in coordination, Cleveland Metroparks offers a slew of Try-It and Learn-It sailing courses: Crewing, Sailing Skills for Crew, Skippering, The STEM of Sailing (Science, Technology, Engineering, Math), Knots To Know on the Water, Sailing Sunset Tours, and more.

OTHER STUFF

Netflix documentary, *Untold: The Race of the Century.* If you ever get yourself to Newport, Rhode Island—which is where this documentary takes place—I highly recommend fresh, raw shucked oysters on the rooftop of Midtown Oyster Bar, hiking Sachuest Point National Wildlife Refuge and after the bars close, skinny-dipping at Third Beach.

One of the ancillary benefits of writing and publishing a book is that I get to set a goal and put it in print as a clever (masochistic?) way to hold myself accountable. This is not a SMART Goal with a specific date, just a regular old goal I want to do before I die:

My goal is to volunteer to be part of a crew on a sleek sailboat racing in the Mills Cup Race—the premier sailing race in Lake Erie. And the stretch-goal would be Susan getting the invite to crew, too.

DeYOUNG

FISH STEELHEAD ALLEY

AT A GLANCE

GREAT LAKES FLY FISHING
@greatlakesflyfishingllc

COVERED BRIDGE OUTFITTERS
@coveredbridgeoutfitters

SALT: A WORLD HISTORY
Mark Kurlansky

THE BIG OYSTER: HISTORY ON THE HALF SHELL
Mark Kurlansky

COD: A BIOGRAPHY OF THE FISH THAT CHANGED THE WORLD
Mark Kurlansky

OUTSIDE MAGAZINE
Last Days of Steelhead Joe by Ian Frazier

THE ESSENTIAL OYSTER
Rowan Jacobsen

FISHERS ISLAND OYSTER FARM
@fishersislandoysters

PADDLE-TO-THE-SEA
Holling C. Holling

SEVEN FIRES: GRILLING THE ARGENTINE WAY
Francis Mallmann with Peter Kaminsky

STEELHEAD GUIDE, FLY FISHING TECHNIQUES AND STRATEGIES FOR LAKE ERIE STEELHEAD
John Nagy

← *(L) 155 Steps Later, The Rocky River*
Gabe Leidy

(R) 'Dream Double 2' painting
Derek DeYoung
curated by Mike Durkalec

A note to West Coast anglers, aquatic biologists and author Mark Kurlansky: Yes, we are well aware our migratory rainbow trout aren't anadromous—and we call 'em *Steelhead* anyway.

Each year, around 400,000, nine-inch Steelhead are stocked in five northern Ohio tributaries: Vermillion River, Rocky River, Chagrin River, Grand River, Conneaut Creek. Affectionately called Steelhead Alley, these five are part of the constellation of tributaries that flow into Lake Erie from its southern shores in Ohio, Pennsylvania, and New York. Sidebar: fingers crossed that someday the Cuyahoga River will receive some baby Steelhead, too.

NEWS FLASH, January 3, 2024: On *The Great Lakes Dude* Podcast with Jeff Liskay, guest and Cleveland Metroparks Aquatic Biologist, Mike Durkalec, revealed that both Steelhead and Sturgeon are going to be stocked in the Cuyahoga in 2024.

After a couple summers in Lake Erie, the Steelhead return home to the rivers where they were *born*. All grown up as world-class gamefish, they titillate anglers with blistering, powerful runs, and cartwheeling acrobatics. Thanks to this annual stocking program, we have some of the most consistent Fall and Spring runs of Steelhead on the planet. And our Steelhead aren't small.

I'd estimate this year my clients and I have caught 100 Steelhead over twenty-eight inches, and quite a few thirty-two inchers, which are monsters—Great Lakes Fly Fishing owner, guide and Patagonia fly fishing ambassador Jeff *Steelhead Junkie* Liskay.

Some Steelhead fishing is done walking/wading a river. Some Steelhead fishing is done using spinning rods or fly rods. Some anglers practice catch and release, believing like famed angler Lee Wulff that *Gamefish are too valuable to be caught only once*. Others fish for the fridge and grill or smoke their Steelhead filets (Robin Wall Kimmerer's "Braiding Sweetgrass", the honorable harvest chapter—*kill quick, give thanks*)

Socrates and I did a float trip on a local river with Captain Cooper Nash, one of the great guides on John Fabian's team at Covered Bridge Outfitters. The trip had a couple firsts: we'd never been in waders and we'd never fished for Steelhead.

And thank our lucky stars we caught some because Captain Coop could finally relax; I guess some clients can be *interesting* when they don't catch fish. But what Coop didn't know is that Socrates and I are happy campers when we're on the water together—whether or not we catch fish.

OTHER STUFF

Mark Kurlansky writes great books: *Salt, The Big Oyster, Cod.* Another outstanding book on oysters is *The Essential Oyster* by Rowan Jacobsen (while he was on his gap year, Michael worked at Fishers Island Oyster Farm; along with the founders Steve and Sarah Malinowski, Michael and crew are in one of the books photos on page 137). Hometown author Ian Frazier wrote a poignant piece for *Outside Magazine* called "Last Days of Steelhead Joe."

COAST OHIO'S LAKE ERIE BIRDING TRAIL—WITH MERLIN

AT A GLANCE

MERLIN BIRD ID
Identify Birds you see & hear

HEARTWOOD COFFEE ROASTERS
46 Ravenna St Suite D-2, Hudson

OHIO LAKE ERIE BIRDING TRAIL
Ohio Department of Natural Resources

BELT MAGAZINE
Warblers and BWIAB piece by Matt Stansfield

← (L) Prothonotary warbler in town for *The Biggest Week in American Birding.* Magee Marsh Wildlife Area
Gabe Leidy

↓ (Below) Warbler
David Wilson | @downpourdw

After the reporter's segment ended, I shot a text to Leslie—a dear friend and one of my favorite dance partners—and asked if she knew anything about the Great Backyard Bird Count (GBBC). The reporter was interviewing folks who sounded like happy drunks confessing their love for the GBBC and some app called *Merlin.*

I'm all over that my friend! Do it every year!

Sometimes I do the Audubon Christmas Bird Count. And the Merlin is the most amazing app in the entire world.

I love being still in nature with my listening and watching senses tuned to high. Birds are everywhere on this planet and even if they're in your backyard, there's a story to be told if you watch closely enough. Birds are flying dinosaurs for goodness sake! Legit! They are remarkable, smart and beautiful. And I could keep going.

A note on Leslie's enthusiasm—it's emblematic of the magical moments when people first dial me in on their microadventures. I remember fondly the first time I spoke to Don Howdyshell and his love for whitewater kayaking the Cuyahoga, Black, and Tinker's Creek—especially after a big rain event. Ditto the stoke of Anthony Smith for whitewater packrafting and mountain biking, Ashley and Rachel at Cleveland Metroparks for hiking the Buckeye Trail's Little Loop, the Skelton Brothers for surfing Lake Erie, and Jeff Liskay, Jessica Suvak, Jess Gantos, and Jimmy Lampros and their love for fly fishing the world-class fisheries we have in northern Ohio. Leslie's unrestrained exhilaration for birding had the same effect on me as theirs—infectious.

Next thing I know, Susan and I are meeting Leslie at Heartwood Coffee Roasters in Chagrin Falls. She gives us a big, fat gorgeous book titled Ohio's *Lake Erie Birding Trails,* loans us a couple pairs of binoculars, instructs us to download the Merlin app and with our Heartwood Honey Buzzes in hand, drives us to South Chagrin Reservation's Jackson Field to participate in our very first GBBC.

OTHER STUFF

Not only do we reside within the region known as Steelhead Alley and call northern Ohio home to the Walleye Capital of the World, it's also home to the Warbler Capital of the World, which hosts the Biggest Week in American Birding (BWIAB) at Magee Marsh Wildlife Area. Hometown boys, Matt Stansfield, along with art from David Wilson, have a great piece in *Belt Magazine* on the birding culture, warblers and the BWIAB; search on *Welcome to the Warbler Capital of the World.*

(L) Blood mane. Eastern Coyote ➙
at Cleveland Lakefront Nature Preserve
Gabe Leidy

(R) Short Earred Owl coasting
the southern shores of Lake Erie
Matt Shiffler

KITEBOARD CONNEAUT

AT A GLANCE

 BREAKWALL BBQ
1205 1/2 Mariana Dr, Conneaut

 FAIRPORT HARBOR CREAMERY
202 High St, Fairport Harbor

 REAL WATERSPORTS
25706 North Carolina Hwy 12, Waves, NC

← *Hang-time at Edgewater*
Kim Karbon

If you're itching to learn how to kiteboard Lake Erie's Conneaut Harbor (or Edgewater Beach, etc), head to Waves, North Carolina.

Every other microadventure in this book can be learned here at home. Want to learn to climb Whipps Ledges? Head to a local climbing gym. Want to learn how to MTB CVNP's Lamb Loop? Head to Ray's Indoor MTB. Kiteboarding? Plan B.

Kiteboarding presents a learning curve that requires not just dedication, but ideally a lesson *center* infrastructure (e.g., jet ski for on-the-fly coaching and rescue). Cooper and I tried learning on our own—FUBAR. The most efficient and safest way to become a kiteboarder is at REAL Watersports on the Outer Banks. Coop and I attended their *Zero to Hero* camp. Father and son had a blast learning, shredding and bonding together.

Conneaut Harbor is a flat water area due to a two-mile break wall. Even as the wind howls above, the water inside the breakwall is often smooth shredding, slick, like *buttah*. The setting is enhanced with a sandbar—providing ample room and shallow waters to launch your kite. And you don't have far to schlep your gear—you can park on the beach. And if you're hungry for more (and proficient staying upwind and performing water re-starts), shoot the gap in the breakwall, and head out to the BIG H_2O.

Nearby Breakwall BBQ for smoked brisket. On your way home, take a short detour for a boozy milkshake at Fairport Harbor Creamery.

OTHER STUFF

Perch & Pilsner Festival. WWII Reenactment. In nearby Ashtabula, Wine & Walleye Festival. While your arms will be *jelly* after your kiteboarding session, Conneaut Creek is a Steelhead Alley tributary. Pack your fishing gear for some Steelhead fishing. Wendell Mueller,* a stranger then, a friend now, guided me to a spot nearby where you can fish from the banks for not only Steelhead, but smallmouth bass, white bass, yellow perch, walleye, pike, catfish, and the under-appreciated freshwater drum.

*At age seventy, Wendell tried something for the first time—he bought a windsurfer. He headed to Wendy Park and New London and learned to windsurf with help from the small but stoked community of Lake Erie windsurfers, kiteborders, and foilers. Yes, you'll spot kiteborders at Edgewater Beach, too.

Edgewater Beach
Kim Karbon

AT A GLANCE

 CENTURY CYCLES
1621 Main St, Peninsula

 WINKING LIZARD
1615 Main St, Peninsula

 TACO TONTOS
123 Franklin Ave, Kent

 MIKE'S PLACE
1700 S Water St #4447, Kent

 JIM'S OPEN KITCHEN TOO
9086 OH-14, Streetsboro

 JOE'S BARBECUE
1290 Tallmadge Rd, Kent

 STAR WALK 2
Constelllation Star Finder App

 THE PHONE BOOTH IN MR HIROTA'S GARDEN
Heather Smith and Rachel Wada

 NIGHTSWIMMING
R.E.M

← *@dirtroadrabbit about to vanish in a dark, dark wood*
Maggie Livelsberger | @large_marge03

*Tonight we ride, right or wrong.
Tonight we sail, on a radio song...Tom Petty*

Soon as it gets dark, we're gonna have us a time
"Choctaw Bingo", James McMurty

If you've only biked the Towpath Trail during the day, a night ride is a nifty twist on the same trail. For decades, Century Cycles has coordinated group night rides on the Towpath. All you need for this free microadventure are bikes, helmets, and headlights. Vintage bikes, cruisers, eBikes, MTB's, fat bikes, gravel bikes, tandems, recumbents, and all skill levels are welcome. Century Cycles can rent you a bike, too.

Rides start at eight PM at Century Cycles in Peninsula. The ride north to Station Road is about fourteen miles, south to Botzum is about thirteen miles. If your legs start barking, turn around, and head back. These are flat miles and take an hour and a half to two hours with many folks heading afterwards to The Winking Lizard for a cold one.

Consider timing your ride to catch the Holy Trinity (golden hour, sunset, blue hour) at Beaver Marsh or Indigo Lake. Twofer hint: full moons rise at sunset. (True darkness is 70-100 minutes after sunset). The Akron Bike Club and Slow Roll Cleveland have night rides, too. There are more out there as well.

If you're keen on a shorter night ride and without the Peloton, there are countless paved trails in our backyard. Here's an incomplete list of pedal-only-as-far-as-you-want, out-n-backs (with one loop thrown in):

- Your own neighborhood
- Portage Park's Trail Lake Park—a rolling 1.6 mile loop. Nearby hike: Nature Conservancy's Herrick Fen Trail. After the ride, hit Taco Tontos for a baked burrito. If it's a morning ride, breakfast at Mike's Place in Kent or Jim's Open Kitchen Too in Streetsboro. Don't forget Joe's BBQ.
- Portage Hike & Bike Trail from Kent's John Brown Tannery Park or Towners Woods (The Battleground)
- Freedom Trail from Middlebury Trailhead
- Summit Metroparks Bike & Hike Trail from SR 303 trailhead towards Brandywine Falls (Boston Ledges)
- Cleveland Metroparks *Emerald Necklace* All-Purpose trails (miles of choices)

OTHER STUFF

Flip the script and experience the duality of a night ride in Cleveland. A night ride in rural, sleepy CVNP versus the urban restlessness of biking the Sokolowskis Loop—one by starlight, the other illuminated by lit bridges and downtown lights. Star Walk 2 app.

MTB CUYAHOGA VALLEY

AT A GLANCE

 RAY'S INDOOR MTB PARK
9801 Walford Ave, Cleveland

 CENTURY CYCLES
1621 Main St, Peninsula

 EDDY'S BIKE SHOP
3707 Darrow Rd, Stow

 BLIMP CITY BIKE & HIKE
1675 Merriman Rd, Akron

 ALL-ROUND CYCLERY
46 Ravenna St ste c-5, Hudson

 THIRSTY DOG BREWING CO.
587 Grant St, Akron

 HiHO BREWING CO
1707 Front St, Cuyahoga Falls

 MARKET GARDEN BREWERY
1947 W 25th St, Cleveland

 FAT HEAD'S BREWERY
17450 Engle Lake Dr, Middleburg Heights

 NORKA
Pick up in store

 INN AT BRANDYWINE FALLS
8230 Brandywine Rd, Northfield

 HOPPIN' FROG BREWERY
1680 E. Waterloo Rd, Akron

← (L) Jay Miller airborn on a Stingray

(R) Keith Miller aloft on a Fuel EX
Jeremy Bryner

Hear her calling—come to me
Thought of her won't let me be
Go to the valley, climb the hill
Whatever it takes darling, you know I will
"Heavy Soul", The Black Keys

If you spent the winter-months inside, learning to mountain bike (MTB) at Ray's Indoor MTB Park, it's time to hit the four MTB trail systems in Cuyahoga Valley.

1. Summit Metro Parks Hampton Hills MTB Area (Swensons, Skyline Chili, Shawarma Brothers)
2. Bedford Reservation Mountain Bike Trails (Gourmands, Lox, Stock & Brisket)
3. Ohio & Erie Canal Reservation Mountain Bike Trails—and bodacious Cleveland-Cliffs Bike Park with pump track, competition course, jump line (The Crispy Chick, Asiatown gems, Slymans Deli Downtown)
4. CVNP's East Rim MTB Trail and Lamb Loop MTB Trail (Russo's, The Farmers Rail, Flip Side, 3 Palms Pizzeria, Downtown 140, Dave's Cosmic Subs)

Thanks to the Conservancy for CVNP, the National Park Service, and Cleveland Area Mountain Bike Association (CAMBA), when the East Rim MTB Trail opened, it was the first official MTB trail in a National Park. While you're there, check out nearby CVNP Countryside Farms: Purplebrown Farm Store, Spicy Lamb Farm, Trapp Family Farm (we buy eggs here).

CAMBA coordinates group MTB rides, ladies-only rides and campouts. Century Cycles, Eddy's Bike Shop, Blimp City Bike and Hudson's All Around Cyclery (and Brent has cold beer) have MTB's and MTB expertise.

Favorite cold beer after a schweddy summertime singletrack session? It's a toss up: Thirsty Dog BloodHound Orange IPA, HiHO's Bossy Lady, Market Garden Brewery Lemon Shandy, Fat Heads Sunshine Daydream IPA. Non-alcoholic thirst-quencher? A cold NORKA root beer (NORKA: AKRON spelled backwards).

We're damn lucky to have so miles of MTB trails in northern Ohio—with more on the way.
1. Atchinson/Hogback Ridge North
2. Austin Badger
3. Big Creek Park
4. Camp Tuscazoar
5. Lake Milton State Park
6. Huffman/Reagan Park (pump track)
7. Mohican State Park
8. Punderson State Park (winter fat biking)
9. Quail Hollow
10. Royalview at Mill Stream Run Reservation
11. Vultures Knob
12. West Branch State Park
13. West Creek Reservation

OTHER STUFF

Stay at the Inn at Brandywine Falls and hit all four Cuyahoga Valley MTB trails. We love staying in their Loft and requesting the Greta Garbo "I vant to be alone" breakfast service.

Cleveland-Cliffs Bike Park at Cleveland →
Metroparks Ohio & Erie Canal Reservation
Photo Courtesy of Cleveland Metroparks

67

SWEEP ROW THE CUYAHOGA

AT A GLANCE

CLEVELAND ROWING FOUNDATION
1003 British St, Cleveland

SAINATO'S AT RIVERGATE
1852 Columbus Rd, Cleveland

@TRASHFISH_CLE
Clean up the river Instagram

@PHASTARCORP
Clean up the river Instagram

BOYS IN THE BOAT
Daniel James Brown

BOYS IN THE BOAT
George Clooney

← *...and sweep row the Portage Lakes;*
Portage Lakes Rowing Association
Meghan Winkler,
courtesy of Akron Life Magazine

When my dad crossed the midlife threshold, he didn't act out like they do in the movies and chase after his youth by buying a sports car and embarking on an extramarital affair—instead, he started sweep rowing the Cuyahoga River.

If you ever give sweep rowing a try, you'll never forget the first time your crew shell is forced to make way for a cargo ship working the Cuyahoga. An eight person shell is sixty-two feet long and the Great Lakes freighter Sam Laud is 615-feet long. When Kacey Musgraves saw the Sam Laud during her 2019 Nautica show she exclaimed, *Holy shit! Thats a big fuckin' boat!*

In addition to kayaks and Stand Up Paddleboards (SUP), the lower section of the Cuyahoga has a growing community sweep rowing the Flats. Eight rowers (plus one coxswain) row boats called *shells*. Rowers row with a single oar called *sweep rowing* and the rowing team is the *crew*. (One rower + two oars = sculling). Rowing presents a learning curve that requires dedication but the spirit of community in the crew shells and boathouse is the essence of collective effervescence. So is the *swing*.

The Cleveland Rowing Foundation has a facility at Rivergate Park which their partner Western Reserve Rowing Association utilizes for their Learn-to-Row (LTR) programs. They also host the annual Head of the Cuyahoga Regatta—one of America's largest.

Nearby and across from Sainatos Pizza is The Foundry. They have the TankHouse with two, state-of-the-art indoor water lanes. Beginners can try the sport by dipping an oar in the pool which generates a current and approximates the sweep rowing experience. Partners in life and business are ordinary miracles and The Foundry has Gina and Mike Trebilcock. Their generosity, passion and commitment to make both rowing and sailing accessible to all deserves a book of its own.

Additional local rowing opportunities: Cleveland Dragon Boats. Portage Lakes Dragon Dream Team. Portage Lakes Rowing Association.

OTHER STUFF

Volunteer to keep the Cuyahoga clean with Eddie Olschansky @trashfish_cle (he'll loan you a kayak) and Canalway Partners for their annual RiverSweep. @phastarcorp is out on the Cuyahoga, too, keeping the river clean and paddlers safe. *Boys in the Boat* by Daniel James Brown. Ditto, the movie, *Boys in the Boat* directed by George Clooney.

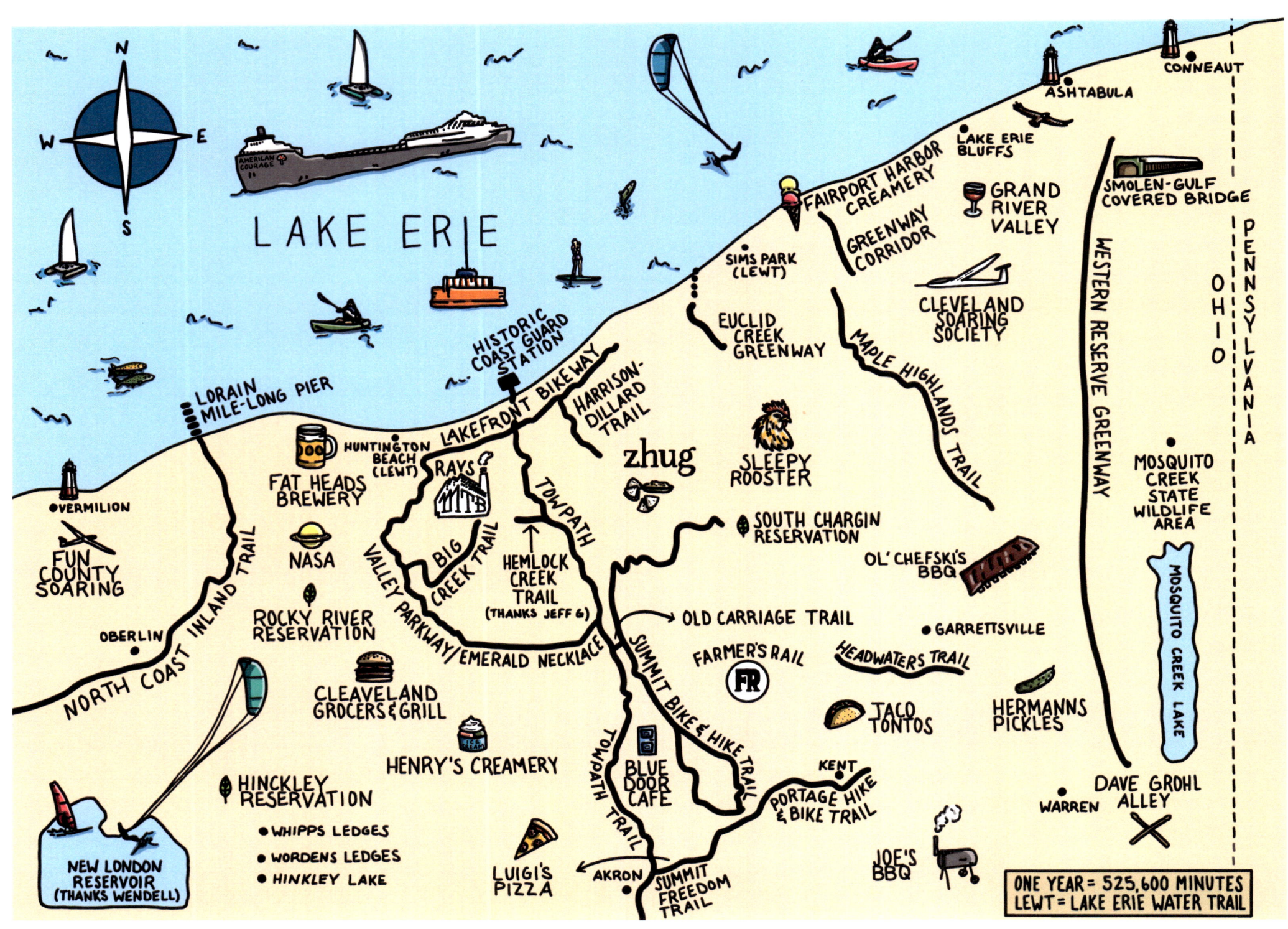

eBIKE THE WESTERN RESERVE

← *Sarah Schmitz*

Nostalgia—it's delicate, but potent. Teddy told me that in Greek nostalgia literally means "the pain from an old wound." It's a twinge in your heart far more powerful than memory alone. This device isn't a spaceship, it's a time machine. It goes backwards, forwards, takes us to a place where we ache to go again. It's not called the wheel. It's called the carousel. It lets us travel the way a child travels. Round and around, and back home again, to a place where we know we are loved.—Mad Men's Don Draper pitching the Kodak Carousel Slide Projector.

With a couple tweaks, this could be a rock-solid pitch for an electric bike. And the sentiment *Nostalgia—it's delicate, but potent* resonates: there's a place I ache to go again.

When Cooper was killed, Jay—a complete stranger then, a friend now—lent me his electric bike (eBike) for the summer. Jay's kindness and eBike were powerful medicine in tending to the sudden, unexpected and traumatic grief of Coop's out-of-order death. But I keep hearing folks chirping that riding an eBike is *cheating*.

At the Newport Folk Festival in 1965 Bob Dylan plugged-in and went electric—and royally pissed off purists expecting his acoustic guitar. Dylan shrugged it off—and changed music history that day. To the acoustic bike purists, Michael Pollan has a good book: *How to Change Your Mind.*

Since I got an eBike of my own, I haven't ridden my acoustic bike. I ride more often (almost daily/nightly). And when I ride, I ride further. Pedaling an eBike connects me to the freedom and exhilaration of those carefree days aboard the Schwinn bicycles of my youth: my green Sting-Ray, red Chicago Cruiser and baby blue Continental. And for a little while, I'm that kid again.

The map on the other page? John Pana helped me make it. As Doug Trattner is to local restaurants, John Pana is to bike trails in the Western Reserve. Like Doug, John is a regional treasure. His journalism, YouTube videos and collection of rides posted on the *Ride With GPS* app guided me to every single northern Ohio bike trail. (One exception: Jeff G for Hemlock Creek Trail.)

OTHER STUFF

Stupid or ignorant? Don't be. When you're riding your eBike and approaching a hiker or slower biker from behind, ring your bell a couple times, holler *passing on your left*, give 'em a brake and as you pass, a friendly *thank you* is always a Midwest nice thing to do. eBikes aren't just for recreating, eBikes can transport you to the big trails, to lunch, to school, to the grocery store—and to work (no sweat). I drive to Peninsula, park the car and pedal the eBike on the Towpath to the day-job in Akron. Bicycle-Themed movies: *Pee Wee's Big Adventure* (1985), *The Bicycle Thief* (1949). An interesting book: David Byrne's, *Bicycle Diaries.*

Abby is one of my closest childhood friends. She and Gary had this Harry Gray gem in their 1993 wedding program. I knew I saved it for a reason.

Most of us miss out on life's big prizes. The Pulitzer. The Nobel. Oscars. Tonys. Emmys. But we're all eligible for life's small pleasures. A pat on the back. A kiss behind the ear. A four-pound bass. A full moon. An empty parking space. A crackling fire. A great meal. A glorious sunset. Hot soup. Cold beer. Don't fret about copping life's grand awards. Enjoy its tiny delights. There are plenty for all of us.

I'd like to add two more tiny delights: dawn patrolling a sunrise and taking a nap. As in, wake up with the stars, watch a luminous sunrise, eat breakfast at the Blue Door Café and then crawl back into bed for a nap.

While I appreciate each and everyone of you that backed this book, honest to God and hand-to-heart, I don't want to be running into any of you on dawn patrols. So it's a no-go on sweet spots to watch the sun rising over the Cuyahoga River Valley.

Instead, this is the story of a lightscape painted by a hockey goalie turned renowned luminist painter—and how it found its way into this book. It all starts and ends with Maxwell's Godmother, Katie.

Katie has known about this book since the early days. In 2021 I was sharing microadventure stories that needed to be paired with photos. When I mentioned "Dawn Patrol Cuyahoga Valley", Katie paused a beat and said, *I think a friend of mine did a painting called Cuyahoga Dawn*. Interesting. I'd never considered an image of a painting for the book—but what the hell, it had *Cuyahoga Dawn* in the title and Katie said she'd ask *Hannock* if I could use it; the name didn't ring a bell.

A year passed and I'd forgotten all about it until Katie said *Cuyahoga Dawn* might be coming to Cleveland as a permanent art installation. And she gave me two books: one titled *Stephen Hannock*, the other *Luminosity*. That night I went down the Stephen Hannock rabbit hole and discovered fast that when it comes to painting, *Hannock* is no weekend-warrior.

Steven Hannock is internationally known as one of the foremost contemporary American luminists. I don't know who Barbara Novak is but she says *In lay parlance, any painting in which light is the most expressive feature may be called luminist*. And, Hannock, along with the the film's technical crew for *Special Visual Effects*, won an Academy Award for the film, *What Dreams May Come*, starring Robins Williams.

In the *Stephen Hannock* art book there's a foldout page with his lightscape painting, *Northern City Renaissance*, which was commissioned by the rock star, Sting. A Hannock Instagram post noted that it was *My fifth in a series of vistas-with-text of Newcastle and Gateshead in Northeastern England; the "everyman" of post-industrial cities...on steroids. As the painting illuminates the course that empires take, we can appreciate a city that has taken the hits, but is clearly on the mend*. I wondered if *Cuyahoga Dawn* would be illuminating the same sentiment—industrial cities coming back on the wings of culture.

← On dawn patrol for freshwater drum on the fly with Jeff Liskay and Socrates

Another year passed and then on May 18, 2023, Katie sent me a text saying *You can use an image of the painting.* I got to the see Stephen's painting for the first time the next day when the file containing a high-resolution image arrived: *Cuyahoga Dawn for Dan Hodermarsky.*

Not only did it have *Cuyahoga Dawn* in the title, the vista-with-text depicted across Stephen's huuuge canvas captured the entire Land of the Connecticut Western Reserve—which is where all these northern Ohio microadventures take place. And that luminous liminal space, that threshold between night and day with the light of dawn spilling across the land and water, was magically and mysteriously stilling. When I saw it, I knew it belonged in this book.

As I found myself doing over the very same landscape while soaring a mile-high in a sailplane with Matterhorn Mike—I took in the views of Stephen's lightscape. An aerial perspective of the land, the Cuyahoga River and Lake Erie, with incandescent flares signaling buried treasures hiding in plain sight—his stories. This is how I inhabited Stephen's painting—by reading it.

Inlaid with handwritten text, it was full of historical, biographical and autobiographical stories of friends and family and the painter's relationship to the land I call home. James Taylor and Jackson Brown, Bruce and Patti, Sting and Trudie, Chrissie Hynde, the Rock-n-Roll HOF, Ozzie Newsome, Paul Newman, Katie, Yo Yo Ma, LeBron at St Vincent-St Mary, Toni Morrison, Ian *Sandy* Frazier, the Underground Railroad, and *On 9/11 as planes flew into the buildings at the end of our street we got the call alerting us to Bridget's brain tumor. A very bad day.* I heard a melancholic echo from one of the art books when I read that.

I dug out the *Stephen Hannock* book and discovered a painting titled *Heroic Woman*—a portrait of his wife, Bridget, pregnant with their daughter, Georgia. Another stilling moment.

Thank you for your art and light and generosity, Stephen; stoked you hung up your goalie gear and skated to where the mystery is going to be. Thank you, Katie, for bringing me a holy trinity moment: synergy, serendipity, synchronicity.

Mitákuye Oyás'iŋ

Cuyahoga Dawn for Dan Hodermarsky →
(Mass MoCA #320), 2020 polished mixed media
(Oil & alkyd, over acrylic and collage) on canvas 64 ½ x 96 ½ in.
Stephen Hannock

FISH THE WALLEYE CAPITAL OF THE WORLD

AT A GLANCE

 GREAT LAKES FLY FISHING
@greatlakesflyfishingllc

 GREAT LAKES BREWING
2516 Market Ave, Cleveland

 COVERED BRIDGE OUTFITTERS
@coveredbridgeoutfitters

 THE DRAKE MAGAZINE
Let the People Fish—Jess Gantos

 **THE DRAKE MAGAZINE**
Biggie Smalls—Jimmy Lampros

 THE FOUNDING FISH
John McPhee

 GREAT LAKES BREWING
Dortmunder Gold™ Lager
Great Lakes IPA
@glbc_cleveland

 KEEPFISHWET.ORG

← *"Walleye"*
   Derek DeYoung

We're not getting into a pissing match about whether Lake Erie is the Walleye Capital of the World. All I'll say is if you're fishing for the fridge, Walleye is some of the finest tasting fish around. And our southern shores of Lake Erie provide some of the most abundant and consistent Walleye fishing on Earth. Full stop.

Disclaimer: Until Socrates and I learn an advanced fly fishing technique—*double hauling* to cast a bare minimum of 30 feet—we've been encouraged to postpone this microadventure.

We had such a fine time fly fishing for freshwater drum with Jeff Liskay at Great Lakes Fly Fishing, we've decided to fish for walleye on the fly with him, too. His vibe, stoke and multi-species knowledge is a regional treasure—Jeff is a tireless steward, a patient teacher, and a MacGyver-like waterman.

Yes, Jeff's passion is fly fishing but if you're not feeling so fly, Jeff has conventional gear, too. Either way, chances are you'll catch Walleye and it's hard to beat beer-battered Walleye made with Great Lakes Dortmunder Gold or some Lake Erie Fish Tacos paired with a Great Lakes IPA.

Another distinctive layer to fishing with Jeff: if you limit out early on Walleye, Jeff can switch gears and get you fishing for a pair of really rowdy fish: freshwater drum and one of Lake Erie's sportiest gamefish—Smallmouth Bass (aka Smallies). Many anglers boast Lake Erie is one of the top places on Earth to fish for trophy Smallies.

If boats make you queasy, local guide Jimmy Mucci with Covered Bridge Outfitters, can put you on breakwalls, piers or knee-deep in the flats with Cleveland's skyline as backdrop. Jimmy swears our homewaters provide *the best smallmouth action in the world.* If you catch 'em, give the gift that keeps on giving: gently release that Smallie to fight another angler on another day. (keepfishwet.org)

OTHER STUFF

Port Clinton Walleye Festival. Ashtabula Wine & Walleye Festival. Local writers and anglers wrote pieces for *The Drake Magazine*: Jess Gantos, "Let the People Fish" and Jimmy Lampros, "Biggie Smalls." Not a local but a damn fine writer, too, John McPhee's *The Founding Fish.*

INOCULATE HIDDEN WATERFALLS

AT A GLANCE

 LNT.ORG
Outdoor Ethics Website

 HIHO BREWING CO.
1707 Front St, Cuyahoga Falls

 HERMANN PICKLE FARM
11964 State Route 88, Garrettsville

 HEARTWOOD COFFEE ROASTERS
20 North Main St. Chagrin Falls

 GOOSETOWN: RECONSTRUCTING AN AKRON NEIGHBORHOOD
Joyce Dyer

← *RIP hidden waterfall*
Nick Hoeller

As we climbed over the mudcatcher below a pair of off-trail CVNP waterfalls, an OG (seasoned) hiker asked if we were *ignorant or stupid*. She was looking at our dry sneakers (we didn't have hiking shoes, yet). She figured (correctly) we hadn't creek-walked the falls—instead we'd trampled the banks.

What's the difference between ignorant and stupid?

☛ Ignorant: not knowing any better and doing it (noob, kook)

☛ Stupid: knowing better but doing it anyway (asshole, shithead)

We used to be those noobs. Kooks chasing off-trail waterfalls, trampling the flora. Hell, we used to build cairns (stacking rocks). We were clueless about *Leave No Trace* (LNT.org).

2,000,000+ folks visit CVNP annually; that's some heavy pressure and begs the question: do we end up *loving nature to death*—especially when a hidden gem gets a viral infection with our social media posts?

Not counting Ashtabula, Cuyahoga, Geauga, Lake, Lorain, Portage, and Summit county parks, there's over 100 waterfalls in CVNP alone—and most have no designated trails. If we're going off-trail, let's get our feet wet and creek-walk 'em. Most are only ankle deep, but head on a swivel for flash flooding.

Spring is my favorite time to visit waterfalls. Snow melt and spring showers trigger heavy flows (don't pass-up frozen waterfalls, though). Here's an incomplete list of year-round favorites (and one infamous) with designated trails:

1. Big Falls (aka Coppacaw Falls, the given name by Native Americans). Coming soon after the deadbeat Gorge Dam is deconstructed
2. Little Falls via High Bridge Glens. Solid spot to watch Don Howdyshell's annual Cuyahoga Falls Paddle Fest (nearby: HiHO Brewery)
3. Blue Hen and Buttermilk Falls
4. Deer Lick Cave Falls
5. Bridal Veil Falls and Great Falls of Tinker's Creek
6. Cascade and Minnehaha Falls (nearby: Don Hermann & Sons Kosher Dill Pickles)
7. Paine and Chair Factory Falls
8. South Chagrin Reservation waterfalls (nearby: Heartwood for a Honey Buzz and breakfast sammich made with red pepper relish)
9. North Chagrin Reservation Buttermilk Falls
10. Mill Creek, Columbia Beach (during sunset), Days Dam and East & West Cascade Falls

OTHER STUFF

Our OG hiker's final observation: think before we post and tag on socials that hidden waterfall. Or as Jerry and the Dead sing, *Please forget you knew my name, my darlin', Sugaree.*

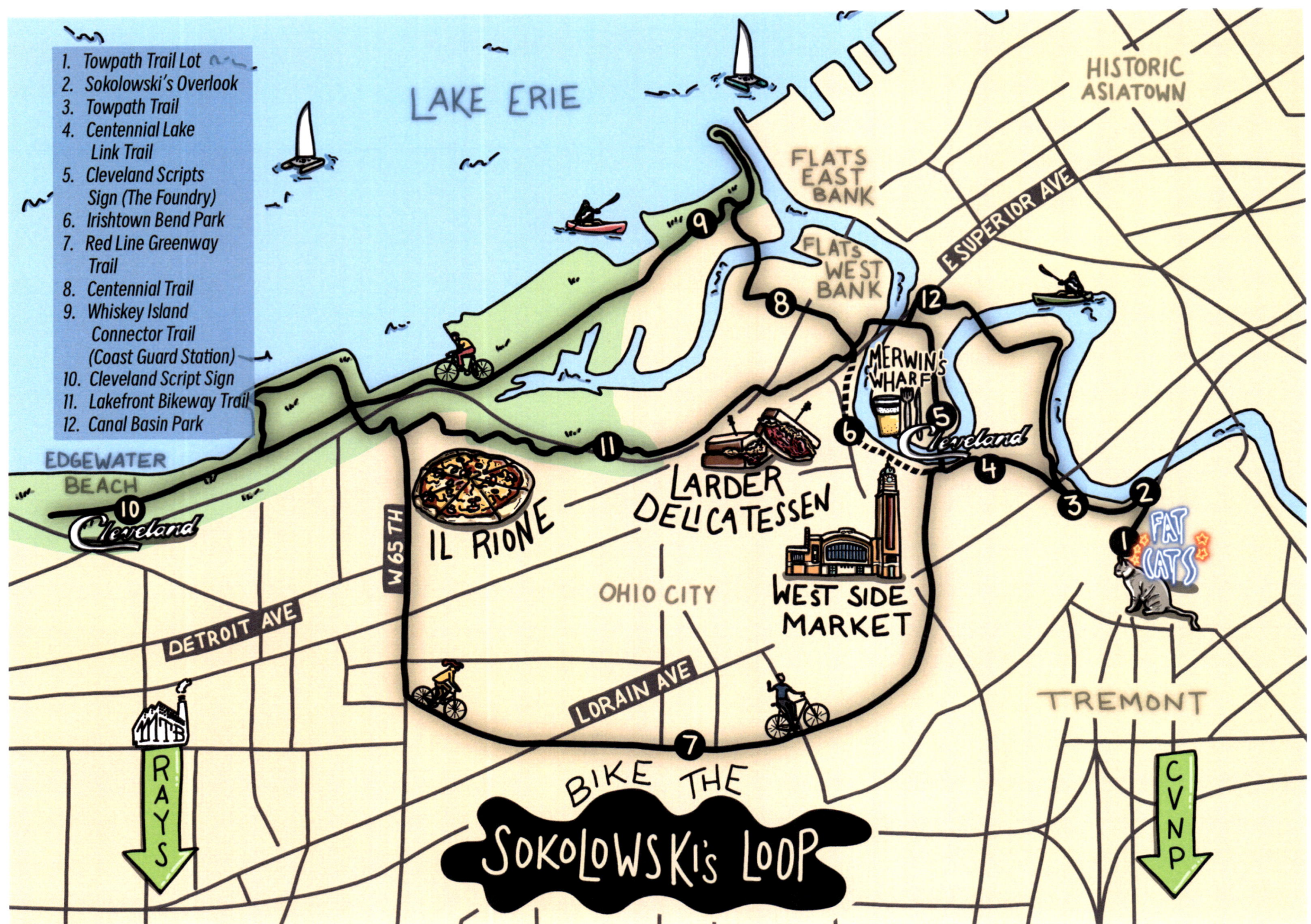

Bike the
SOKOLOWSKI'S LOOP

BIKE THE SOKOLOWSKI'S LOOP

I almost named this overnight microadventure "Bike the Fat Cat's Loop" in honor of Ricardo Sandoval. Ricardo has a sweet set-up that's just off the Towpath in Cleveland's historic Tremont neighborhood: he can feed you *and* give you a place to rest your weary head. Ricardo is the Chef/Owner of Fat Cats, an eclectic restaurant on one floor and upstairs on the other, Ricardo has a bistro apartment suite with skyline views that he Airbnbs.

Fat Cats is busy and busy for a reason—and they've been busy doing their distinctive thing since 1997. If you can't score a rez for Ricardo's home-away-from-home, or pied-à-terre, Aloft and Kimpton Schofield Hotel are solid options (I believe one of them was the former home of the Winfred-Louder department store where comedian and *The Price Is Right* host Drew Carey once worked).

But I named this microadventure "Bike the Sokolowski's Loop" because of my emotional connection to the gone but not forgotten Sokolowski's University Inn—a temple to Polish and Eastern European food and a James Beard Foundation "American Classics" Award-winning restaurant.

High-level, this bike ride is an out-n-back—with a route that looks like deformed figure-eight. It starts on the Towpath at Sokolowski's Overlook, takes you out to the Cleveland Script sign at Edgewater Park and returns you to Sokolowski's Overlook. The nexus, or point of intersection on the figure-eight, is the Center Street Swing Bridge (roughly where routes #5 and #12 intersect). Don't let the presence of the Red Line Greenway Trail (#7) bewilder you as you try to *see*

the figure-eight; I bike this route for a different microadventure and I've referenced it here only to create awareness for this nifty trail.

From Sokolowski's Overlook (#2), you'll drop-in and enjoy a fast, fun downhill before leaving the Towpath (#3) and veering left onto the Centennial Lake Link Trail (#4) and riding it to Columbus Road where you'll need to make a decision: hang a left just past Hoopples and pick up the Red Line Greenway Trail (#7) or turn right and pedal over the Columbus Road Lift Bridge—for this microadventure, hang a right onto route #5.

☛ Soon you'll have a 3rd option: to head straight and pedal through Irishtown Bend Park (#6)—a transformative project underway as I write.

Once you cross the Columbus Road Lift Bridge you'll have an opportunity to do some off-route exploring: Rivergate Park—Hart Crane Memorial Park, Cleveland Metroparks Merwin's Wharf, Cleveland Dragon Boat Association, a rough-n-rowdy skatepark, Ohio City Bicycle Co-op, The Flats Platform Tennis Center, Western Reserve Rowing Foundation, and nearby and cross from Sainato's at Rivergate (pizza, pasta, beer) is The Foundry and TankHouse (peek in the window to see the two indoor water lanes). A Cleveland Script hides behind The Foundry's historic building; ditto what is believed to be the world's longest rowing dock at 521 feet, parallel to the river's edge.

As you continue down route #5 and make a left at the stop sign onto Center Street, you'll pedal past Larry Flynt's Hustler Club, the historic Flat Iron Café (love their chowder, wings, perch, burgers and beer) and Catanese Classic with its robust selection of oysters and other fresh seafood. At this point you're at the nexus of the deformed figure-eight and about to cross the Center Street Swing bridge. From there it's as easy as following #8, #9, #10, #11, and #12 (Canal Basin Park) before pedaling the Towpath through Scranton Flats (I forgot to have Sarah draw this into the map) and up the big hill back to Sokolowski's Overlook.

OTHER STUFF

Cuyahoga, a debut novel by Pete Beatty that spins a hilarious yarn about Ohio City, the City of Cleveland and the fight over a bridge across the Cuyahoga. Flip the script and night-bike the Sokolowski's Loop. Social rides: Slow Roll Cleveland on Monday nights and Bike Cleveland on last Friday nights of the month. Stream: *The Drew Carey Show*—a hometown kid's ode to Cleveland. Paul Newman's (Shaker Heights) *The Last Movie Star*. Alan Ruck (Cleveland) as Cameron in *Ferris Bueller's Day Off*. And while no hometown kids appear in them—if you're a food-lover—stream *Chef* (2014) and *Ratatouille* (2007).

← *Sarah Schmitz*

SURF LAKE ERIE

AT A GLANCE

@LAKESURFISTAS
Women who surf the Great Lakes

LARDER DELI
1455 W 29th St, Cleveland

IL RIONE
1303 W 65th St, Cleveland

GREAT LAKES BREWING
2516 Market Ave, Cleveland

OUT OF PLACE
Scott Ditzenberger

**UNSALTED: A GREAT
LAKES EXPERIENCE**
Vince Deur

STEP INTO LIQUID
Dana Brown

**BARBARIAN DAYS,
A SURFING LIFE**
William Finnegan

← *American Courage*
Gabe Leidy

The Euclid Beach Band's 1979 hit "There's No Surf in Cleveland" is a catchy, pro-Cleveland song, but the band missed the wave—you can surf Lake Erie. And our unsalted home waters ensure you can watch Shark Week the same week you try surfing without any fear you'll end up like Quint's friend *Herbie Robinson from Cleveland*.

True, no one's going to be surfing waves like the giants at Oahu's North Shore, Maui's Pe'ahi (*Jaws*), California's Mavericks or Portugal's Nazaré, but that's the double-barrelled magic of Lake Erie surfing. Surfing Lake Erie is accessible to any adventurous soul. And, surfing Cleveland's Edgewater Beach is a buried treasure not many folks know about—and that tees up the surf-curious for a fancy-schmancy thing called *applied positive psychology.*

Some research suggests a key to pursuing happiness is lowering expectations. As Lake Erie surfer Robin Pacquing @lakesurfistas frames it, *The idea of actual surf doesn't exist here. There's zero expectation—and that breeds this culture of stoked people making do with what they have.*

Researchers *discovered that feeling happy depends not on how well things are going overall, but whether they are going better than expected.* Maybe living without great expectations—"There's No Surf in Cleveland"—was what the song was about all along.

As someone who once ran away to Rhode Island and took a job that would allow me to chase striper and bluefish blitzes and the winds for windsurfing, I have a real affection for our small but stoked surf community. Hearty souls prioritizing their lives so they can obsessively monitor meteorological apps, then race to the beach, squeeze into wetsuits and paddle out into Lake Erie's frigid waters (the surf fires when the wind blows real hard—and that happens when it's real cold).

My shins and knees are still sore from my one-and-only surf session. I'm happy to grab some Koji-cured pastrami perfection from Larder Deli or a pie from Il Rione and watch the Edgewater surfers surf from inside my warm car.

Thirsty for a beer inspired by our local surf scene? Great Lakes Brewing's Chillwave Imperial IPA (ABV 9%).

OTHER STUFF

Watch a pair of Great Lakes surf documentaries (featuring Lake Erie): Scott Ditzenberger's *Out of Place* and Vince Deur's *Unsalted: A Great Lakes Experience.*

CAMP LAKE ERIE BLUFFS

AT A GLANCE

APPALACHIAN OUTFITTERS
60 Kendall Park Rd Suite A, Peninsula

BACKPACKERS SHOP
@thebackpackersshop

FALLS OUTDOOR COMPANY
1727 Front St, Cuyahoga Falls

MERLIN
Identify Birds you see & hear

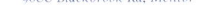
**SCOOTER'S WORLD
FAMOUS DAWG HOUSE**
9600 Blackbrook Rd, Mentor

FAIRPORT HARBOR CREAMERY
202 High St, Fairport Harbor

HERITAGE FARMS
@heritagefarmspeninsula

**VALLEY OVERLOOK
AT CAMP BUTLER**
@visitvalleyoverlook

← ...and camp South Bass
Island State Park, too
Gabe Leidy

Life is beautiful around a campfire—time kinda stops its steady march as you stare into the flames. Lake Metroparks has a respite or two from the hustle & bustle.

Lake Erie Bluffs (LEB) is a popular camping destination, and popular for a reason. Two secluded campsites with panoramic views of Lake Erie and an inland sea lapping (or crashing) on the shores just below your tent, pitched on the bluffs above.

And you're just a few steps away from a couple miles of trails. Trails that will take you to a fifty-foot, coastal observation tower perched above Lake Erie—where on a clear day you can see the Fairport Harbor Lighthouse. And it's lit at night.

LEB is the perfect hack to getting up early at home to drive to dawn patrol a sunrise—you're already outside. Then crawl back in your sleeping bag until the rise-n-shiner in your crew starts grilling up the bacon for a cowboy breakfast. And it's a sublime spot for golden hours, sunsets and blue hours. If you're there on a full moon, as the sun is setting, turn around—the full moon will be rising.

You can swim, kayak, SUP and surf/shore fish along a nearly two-mile beach (there's been some erosion). Prime spot, too, to beachcomb for water-smoothed stones and beach glass.

Camping at LEB is certainly not glamping, but it isn't boondocking, either. While there's no water or electricity, the parking lot is close to each campsite—not far to schlep your gear—and there's washrooms. Gear up at Appalachian Outfitters, The Backpackers Shop, Falls Outdoor Company. Hint: give *hammocking* a try.

Here's some icing on the cake if you're birding-curious: LEB is on Ohio's Lake Erie Birding Trail—an important migratory flyway featuring world-class birding. Raptors like bald eagles and ospreys are regularly seen. And you might get lucky and see or hear a Merlin. Speaking of Merlin, download the Merlin app.

OTHER STUFF

On the way home, Scooter's World Famous Dawg House and Fairport Harbor Creamery for boozy milkshakes. Back home, camp Christmas Tree Farm and Valley Overlook at Camp Mueller.

Don Howdyshell on the →
Upper Gorge, Cuyahoga River
Meghan Winkler courtesy of Akron Life Magazine

RIDE THE RAILS, PADDLE THE RIVER

My good buddy Drob and I missed the train on this one. He'd invited me to kayak Segment Four of the Cuyahoga River Water Trail—a maiden voyage for both. His game plan was to put-in at Peninsula's Lock 29, paddle eight-miles down river north and take-out just before Brecksville Reservation's Station Road Bridge. We worked harder driving and unloading and loading and transferring the kayaks than we did paddling the river—but we didn't know any other way to do it than the following:

We met-up in Peninsula, drove two cars (Drob's had the two kayaks thanks to Linda & Griff) to Brecksville Reservation and dropped my car. We drove back together to Peninsula and put-in. When we finished, we loaded the kayaks into my car and drove back to Peninsula to unload and then load them into his car. The Cuyahoga Valley Scenic Railroad (CVSR) has a program to eliminate much of this loading/unloading/transferring/driving. We'll get to that in a couple seconds.

We had a relaxing and sporty (some modest whitewater) time kayaking together—and a dose of the surreal. We both capsized our kayaks—and Drob's car keys went into the river. We swam our kayaks river-right and began to calmly bail them out on the banks—and startled ourselves by how *not pissed* we were; hell, we were laughing and laughing hard. And in the calm of that moment

the solution was crystal clear: call Drob's most-excellent wife, Julie, and she could meet us with a spare set of keys. And just as we were ready to slide back into our kayaks, Drob's car keys came floating by in the zip-lock bag with an air bubble in it.

Segment 4 of the Cuyahoga River Water Trail is now one of my favorite segments to paddle—and the CVSR is a big reason why. There's no need to drop a second vehicle because the CVSR has a Kayak Program. The CVSR volunteers will load your kayaks on the train—and let 'em ride the rails with ya. We like parking at Brecksville Reservation and riding the rails with our kayaks to Peninsula for the first leg of the journey. That way you can take your time on the river, not stressing about missing the train. You buy your tickets on the train and the CVSR volunteers appreciate cash.

Start the day with breakfast in Independence at Gourmond's (weekdays only) or Yours Truly. Post-paddle, Tinkers Creek Tavern or head south on Riverview Road and catch a sunset at Ledges Overlook or Indigo Lake followed by some oysters, beers and more at Chef Dave Russo's Italian & Cajun joint.

Cleveland Metroparks has *Learn-It* classes for kayaking. Ditto 41 North Coastal Adventures. And likely your local highschool pool does, too.

Packraft the Cuyahoga. While you'll see plenty of kayaks, Socrates and I like the agility, stability and portability of a lightweight, inflatable packraft to paddle the Cuyahoga as well as our other rivers, inland lakes and ponds.

Paddle the River, Pedal the Towpath. A go-anywhere packraft is to adventure on water as a go-anywhere gravel bike is to adventure on land. Combine the two and you're bikerafting. Strap your bike on your packraft, put-in at Peninsula, paddle down the Cuyahoga, take-out at Station Road Bridge, deflate your packraft, pack it on your bike, and pedal the Towpath back to your vehicle in Peninsula.

Whatever you paddle, in addition to a dry bag with a float or a zip-lock bag with an air bubble in it, wear a PFD (personal floatation device), and check water flow. Yes, Julie & Susan, Drob and I had our PDF's on and secured.

Drob—it's time to get that whole hog from Duma Meats, oysters from Fishers Island Oysters, break out the La Caja China and Bulls Bay OYRO Cooker and have ourselves another oyster and hog roast.

OTHER STUFF

Pack a fishing rod. This stretch of the Cuyahoga is teaming with resident Smallmouth Bass. While smaller than Lake Erie's trophy smallies, they're stout, feisty, and plentiful. *Pig Perfect: Encounters with Remarkable Swine and Some Great Ways to Cook Them* by Peter Kaminsky

← *Cuyahoga Valley Scenic Railroad*
Ryan Gryzbowski

↑ *Cuyahoga River portage* | *Meghan Winkler, courtesy of Akron Life Magazine*

Sarah Schmitz

GET LOST IN STEBBINS GULCH

AT A GLANCE

CORDELIA
2058 E 4th St, Cleveland

THAXTON'S ORGANIC GARLIC
2710 Ravenna St, Hudson

MICHAEL SYMON'S CARNIVORE
Michael Symon with Douglas Trattner

CROOKED PECKER BREWING
8284 E Washington St, Chagrin Falls

STEBBINS GULCH
Mary Oliver

← (L to R)

Bacon, **Ohio City Provisions**

Fried Lake Perch, **The Boulevard Tavern**

Fried Chicken, **Cordelia**

Sardine & Rouille, **The Judith**

Smoked Salmon, **Kate's Fish**

Baked Burrito, **Taco Tontos**

Pastrami Sammich, **Larder Deli**

"Cleveland Eats", Written by Douglas Trattner Designed by Brian Barr, Published by Free Period Press

Eat More Meat, **Mabel's BBQ**

TFR Burger, **The Farmer's Rail**

Pie, **Luigi's Pizza**

Mezze, **Zhug**

AB, by Sarah Schmitz

Corned Beef on Rye, **Slymans Original**

Boozy Milkshake, **Fairport Harbor Creamery**

Oysters, **The Blue Door**

The Betty, **Martha On The Fly**

Central Texas Style Brisket, **Joe's BBQ**

Soup Dumplings, **LJ Shanghai**

Pie, **Il Rione**

Anthony Bourdain once described a Guinness pub in Ireland as *gloriously unfucked by time.* Holden Forests & Gardens' Stebbins Gulch is stuck in a similar time warp—no hand of man on these prehistoric grounds.

There's no trash or cairns polluting this thirty million year-old deep ravine environment. You won't see interpretive signs, observation platforms or benches to rest your weary bones. And you won't encounter tourist hordes loving nature to death. It's just you, a few other adventurous souls and your Holden naturalist-guides (Jennifer and Dan on our hike). Stebbins Gulch and its cascades, rock shelters, forest zones, microclimate and Audubon-worthy birding—preserved in all its isolation—reveals another distinctive layer to Northern Ohio.

It's not free—gotta pay to play here. Holden's stewardship adheres to a preservation model that keeps the gulch *unimpaired for the enjoyment of future generations.* Their balancing act between preservation and use is decidedly in the former's favor.

Hell, trying to score a reservation for this rare guided hike can be tougher than a rez at Michael Symon's gone but not forgotten *Lola Bistro.* Speaking of that sacred space—2508 East 4th Street—Andrew Watts' and Chef Vinnie Cimino's *Cordelia* honors that legacy with their Midwest-nice vibe and *Modern Grandma* cuisine.

The Holden property also includes the 500-foot long Murch Canopy Walk and 120-foot tall Kalberer Emergent Tower which perches you above the treetops overlooking Little Mountain—where on a clear day you can see Lake Erie. Speaking of...

Holden has another preserve—some say more magical than Stebbins. Isn't it ironic? As I write this, Holden's website announces *Magnificence on the Mountain*—the rare guided hike through Little Mountain—is *SOLD OUT.*

We road tripped to Chagrin Falls with The Black Keys: Bell & Flower (blood orange margaritas, crispy Nashville hot chicken sammich), Jeni's (ice cream) and Crooked Pecker Brewing for some pickup cans (Accidental Anderson 7.7% ABV).

OTHER STUFF

"Stebbins Gulch"—a poem by Cleveland native and Pulitzer Prize-winning poet Mary Oliver. "Seventh Generation Principle"—an ancient Haudenosaunee (Iroquois) philosophy that says the decisions we make today should result in a sustainable world seven generations into the future. All I had from the Stebbin's Gluch hike was a lame-ass photo of a big-ass burl. Pictured are a few, fave local eats.

SUP THE LAKE ERIE WATER TRAIL

Cleveland Metroparks collaborated with cities along the Cuyahoga County coast to create the Lake Erie Water Trail (LEWT). The twenty-plus mile water trail spans from Huntington Beach on the western edge of Cuyahoga County to Sims Park on the eastern edge. The LEWT currently has thirteen public access points to put-in and take-out your sea kayak or SUP (Stand Up Paddleboard). That's all I'm gonna say about LEWT. This is a story about public access and PPP's.

I was lucky to meet John Debo, Jr recently. John was CVNP's third Park Superintendent. One of the bigger take-aways from our conversation was John's perspective on the increasing importance of *friends of the park* groups.

During John's tenure, Congressman Ralph Regula worked his magic and political might to sustainably provide duly appropriated funds for fledgling CVNP. Those days are long gone—the financial resources just aren't there from the federal government anymore. So where does the vitally needed financial and program support come from for park systems like CVNP, Summit Metro Parks and Cleveland Metroparks? From Public-Private Partnerships (PPP's).

Public CVNP is partnered with private Conservancy for Cuyahoga Valley National Park, a 501(c)(3) non-profit and a friends of the park group. Through their fundraising and philanthropic efforts, the Conservancy purchased for preservation the land of Brandywine Golf Course in Peninsula—and then integrated 198 acres into CVNP.

Western Reserve Land Conservancy (WRLC) purchased the 28.5 acre Euclid Beach Mobile Home Park on North Collinwood's Lake Erie shoreline, which WRLC will transfer to Cleveland Metroparks. (Yes, the residents of the mobile home park will be displaced).

West Creek Conservancy acquired land to support the creation of Irishtown Bend Park—a transformative project that will, among many other achievements, connect the Ohio City community to the waterfront and provide the missing link between the 101-mile Ohio & Erie Canal Towpath Trail and Lake Erie.

The City of Euclid and a hundred citizens/stakeholders along Lake Erie partnered on an inspired PPP that might just serve as a precedent for Cleveland, if not a model for the Great Lakes Region. It was a Win for Euclid City government committed to increasing public access to the lake and a Win for homeowners struggling financially to stop the lake from taking a foot of earth from their shoreline property each year (erosion).

One hundred years ago, F.A. Seiberling and the Olmsted Brothers (renowned landscape architects) identified the Himelright Dairy Farm, nestled along a segment of the Cuyahoga River, as a prime piece of land for preservation. In 2016, Summit Metro Parks completed the strategic acquisition of the dairy farm's second act—the Valley View Golf Club. Today, those 194 acres are re-wilding as the Valley View Area of Cascade Valley Metro Park. The friends of the park were Summit County taxpayers passing a levy.

My first conscious experience with a PPP was with Maxwell in 2010—we were in New York City for his father-son, 10th birthday adventure. Unconsciously, it was another first: exploring that fine line between the wilds and urban living. Thanks to "The Friends of the High Line" 501(c)(3) and the City of New York, nature found a way to wedge itself into NYC's concrete jungle by repurposing an abandoned railroad spur into an elevated linear park, greenway and rail trail. Maxwell and I explored the wilds of the High Line—and feasted on burnt ends, candy salads and deep-fried Oreos (invented in 1912 at the Chelsea Market Bakery). And we promised ourselves "we gonna make it" and beat the line for burgers, shakes and crinkle cut fries at the first Shake Shack, located in Madison Square Park, a short walk from our historic Chelsea Hotel (nope, we didn't see Bob Dylan, Leonard Cohen or any ghostly apparitions).

OTHER STUFF

Conservancy for CVNP, WRLC, West Creek Conservancy, Friends of Metro Parks and other 501(c)(3) non-profits also play potent roles in developing citizen-supported volunteer organizations. The Book of Rewilding: *Practical Guide to Rewilidng, Big and Small*, by Isabella Tree. *Rewilding: The Radical New Science of Ecological Recovery*, by Paul Jepson, Cain Blythe. *Entangled Life* by Merlin Sheldrake. *Mycelium Running* by Paul Stamets. The documentary, *Fungi: Web of Life*, narrated by Icelandic musician-actress Björk Guðmundsdóttir.

← *The 5-Mile Crib, a scenic overlook along the Lake Erie Water Trail (LEWT)*
@ediexplores

LOCAL MUSIC

SKINNY
Alex Bevan—*East Cleveland*

BUSTED
Black Keys—*Dan and Patrick, Akron*

BUT ANYWAY
Blues Traveller—*John Popper, Chardon*

ACROSS 110TH STREET
Bobby Womack—*Cleveland*

CLEVELAND IS THE CITY
Bones Thugs n Harmony—*Cleveland*

LOWDOWN
Boz Scaggs—*Canton*

BY AND BY
Caamp—*Matt Vinson, Hudson*

SATISFACTION
Devo—*Akron*

THERE'S NO SURF IN CLEVELAND
Euclid Beach Band—*Cleveland*

EVERLONG
Foo Fighters—*Dave Grohl, Warren*

PUMPED UP KICKS
Foster the People—*Mark Foster, Macedonia*

CLEVELAND ROCKS
Ian Hunter—*Out-of-towner*

FUNK #49
James Gang—*Cleveland*

OUR HEARTS ARE WRONG
Jessica Lea Mayfield—*Kent*

CLEVELAND IS THE REASON
Kid Cudi—*Cleveland*

MY TOWN
Michael Stanley Band—*Cleveland*

LOVE TRAIN
O'Jays—*Canton*

GET YOUR ASS TO CLEVELAND
Pat Dailey—*Out-of-towner*

BURN ON
Randy Newman—*Out-of-towner*

CUYAHOGA
R.E.M.—*Out-of-towner*

PLUSH
Stone Temple Pilots—*Scott Weiland, Bainbridge Twp*

MY CITY WAS GONE
The Pretenders—*Chrissie Hynde, Akron*

FAST CAR
Tracy Chapman—*Cleveland*

I KNOW WHAT BOYS WANT
Waitresses—*Akron*

*Scan for CVMA
Local Music* ☝

AT A GLANCE

ROCK THIS TOWN! BACKSTAGE
IN CLEVELAND: STORIES YOU
NEVER HEARD AND SWAG
YOU NEVER SAW
Fran Belkin

RUN, BIKE, HIKE, PADDLE, RACE

AT A GLANCE

 BORN TO RUN
Christopher McDougall

 RACES

Headwaters Adventure Race

Ledges to Lake Adventure Race

Whiskey Island Paddlefest

Blazing Paddles Paddlefest

Grand River Canoe and Kayak Race

MammothMarch

← *SUP's and kayaks queueing up for the annual Blazing Paddles Paddlefest
By Drone Ohio for SharetheRiver.com*

When's the last time you competed in a race just for the fun of it? An adrenaline-filled race to the finish line, laughing all the way, not caring whether you won or lost? Maybe it was the sack race on field day in elementary school. Maybe when you and your three best friends raced your bikes down a straight stretch of road, just for the hell of it. What if, as an adult, you could compete in a race and rather than the fear of losing, it was genuinely about having fun—and getting that deep feeling of joy and accomplishment?

Portage Park District's Headwaters Adventure Race is one of many. There are multiple categories like tag-teaming with a partner for the Two Person Relay Team: one person runs two miles on the Headwaters Trail, the other bikes ten miles on rural roads and both paddle five miles on the Upper Cuyahoga Scenic River.

Another popular Run, Bike and Paddle is Cleveland Metroparks Ledges to Lakes Adventure Race at Hinckley Reservation. Grab your Stand Up Paddleboard (SUP) or kayak and race in the Whiskey Island Paddlefest or Blazing Paddles Paddle Fest. Head to Lake Metroparks for the Grand River Canoe and Kayak Race. If you've gotten into MTB (if not, head to Ray's Indoor MTB), check out Cleveland Metroparks Bedford XC MTB Race. The course is perfect for both beginners and advanced riders.

And check out the Mammoth March (NOT A RACE), a twenty mile hiking route through CVNP. Diana at Hudson's Stretchlab just did this and said the math adds up: enjoyment, satisfaction, and meaning equals happiness. Sidebar: Diana and fellow Stretchlab Flexologist, Stacy, were the first practitioners I went to after Cooper was killed. The physical pain of grief ain't a myth.

Here's an incomplete list of other local races where it's more about making memories than medaling.

1. Towpath 50 (biking)
2. Western Reserve Racing's Trilogy Race Series (running, hiking)
3. Bike Cleveland Fundo
4. VeloSano Ride-to-Cure (biking)
5. Road Apple Roubaix (gravel biking)
6. Buckeye Trail Little Loop challenge (hiking)
7. GOBA (Great Ohio Bike Adventure) NOT A RACE. Michael and I did this seven day bike & camp tour when he was ten. He broke his arm before the ride and rode GOBA with a full-arm cast. In 2023 the route was in northeastern Ohio.

OTHER STUFF

Christopher McDougall's *Born to Run: A Hidden Tribe, Superathletes and the Greatest Race the World Has Never Seen.*

(L) Tiller time, Jessica Suvak →

(R) Jessica Suvak, Leslie Gair, and a musky
Jess Suvak

FLOAT A RIVER FOR NORTHERN PIKE

AT A GLANCE

THE FISH'S EYE
Ian Frazier

COVERED BRIDGE OUTFITTERS
@coveredbridgeoutfitters

8TH DAY BREWING COMPANY
11782 Washington St, Chagrin Falls

IN SEARCH OF SMALL GODS
Jim Harrison

**THE LONGEST SILENCE:
A LIFE IN FISHING**
Thomas McGuane

**A RIVER RUNS THROUGH IT
AND OTHER STORIES**
Norman Maclean

**DUMB LUCK AND THE KINDNESS
OF STRANGERS**
John Gierach

TROUT BUM
John Gierach

**WHY FISH DON'T EXIST:
A STORY OF LOSS, LOVE, AND
THE HIDDEN ORDER OF LIFE**
Lulu Miller

← John Fabian and a
Northern Pike on the fly
John Fabian

The Number One Rule of Fight Club is *You Don't Talk About Fight Club*. Like surfers and their surf breaks, anglers don't talk about their honey holes. We'll just say this microadventure takes place on a local river.

Some anglers troll from boats. Some walk/wade. Some surf/shore cast. Socrates and I were in a float boat and the man working the oars was John Fabian, a mensch and Orvis-endorsed, multi-species fishing guide, instructor, and owner of Covered Bridge Outfitters.

As the current pulled us down river, John coached us on tips, tricks and techniques to make ideal presentations to attract a strike from a Northern Pike, the trip's target species. Pike are rocket-shaped ambush predators with mouthfuls of razor-sharp teeth—a hauntingly beautiful species.

Outdoor writers like John Gierach, Norman Maclean, Tom "Captain Beserko" McGuane, Jim Harrison, and Ian Frazier paint sublime scenes of the joy of fly fishing—not just the glory of catching. Viewed from a certain angle, fly fishing becomes imbued with the mystery of a soul-stirring ceremony.

Drifting past beavers, otters, and sandhill cranes with blue herons, eagles and ospreys soaring overhead, life on land turned to vapors. With the longest of silences, we casted and drifted and flowed into a state of calm attentiveness...until a Pike hit, the line tightened, Socrates' rod bent, the dopamine squirted and John and Socrates teamed to fight, net and gently release the rowdy rocket back to the river.

When time was called on our float trip, John fired up the motor and we hauled-ass north, planing up river, carving hairpin turns back to the take-out and a cooler of beers.

The finest gift you can give to any [angler] is to put a good fish back, and who knows if the fish that you caught isn't someone else's gift to you? Lee Wulff

OTHER STUFF

Float a local river with John and Covered Bridge Outfitters for the apex freshwater predator on the fly: Muskellunge (aka Musky). Ian Frazier's *The Fish's Eye*.

104

← *Bass—Deer Hair Popper*
Derek DeYoung

106

FERRY TO PELEE ISLAND

← *Peelee Island*
  Ian Virtue

I have a thing for ferries. But until Susan and I sailed the ferry from Leamington, Ontario, Canada to Pelee Island, I couldn't name it. My friend, and Maxwell's godmother, Katie landed on her *ferry thing* years ago:

It's the same feeling of excitement children have on Christmas morning...the first sensation is smelling the sea air. I watch the ferrymen getting ready to leave the harbor while I head for the top deck to watch the ferry boat pull away from the mainland.

If the weather is bad I've already staked out my area below with my bags knowing they're safe. I usually walk around the upper and lower deck looking at the relaxed but excited faces of my fellow travelers.

After about two hours I return to the bow to watch for the island. As we approach the harbor, the lighthouse, church steeple and gray shingled buildings come into view and I know I'm home.

I was ten when I boarded my first ferry. And the ferry thing showed up on that ride to Ocracoke from mainland North Carolina. Since then, there've been too many ferries to too many islands to trot them all out here. The most meaningful, though? From Point Judith to Block Island—where I asked Susan to marry me.

Since Coop died, some interesting stuff has revealed itself. Philosopher and author Stephen Jenkinson was reflecting on a much different experience, but his description not only gives a name to my ferry thing, but sunrises and sunsets and island time, too.

This is a stilling thing, not a compelling thing. This is an interruption in the normally scheduled programming. This is a willingness to stop, and subsequently slow down—in that order.

Island time on Pelee included:

- The warmth, hospitality and compassion shown by Cathy (Pelee Island Mayor) and Kevin Miller, the InnKeeps of The Wandering Dog Inn.[†]
- Gravel bike rides under still starry skies to dawn patrol sunrises at East Park Beach (shoulda had fat bikes, especially on Cooper Road.)
- Deep-fried Perch and Smelt at The Westview Tavern
- Sunsets at the picnic table across from the west pump station—a sublime setting.
- Brian Selznick's *Big Tree* and Dave Eggers' *The Eyes and the Impossible.* Needed a respite from the grief books.
- Since Coop died, I've found myself on Amazon ordering books from my youth to re-read: *My Side of the Mountain, Where the Red Fern Grows, Zen and the Art of Motorcycle Maintence, City: A Story of Roman Planning and Construction, Way of the Peaceful Warrior.* Comforting escapism.
- And since Coop died, I like to put on the Grateful Dead's "American Beauty" and think about times at the kitchen table with Mrs. Burnham and Shep, getting tutored in Latin & life.

[†]Wandering Dog Inn: We acknowledge we are in the traditional, ancestral home of Caldwell First Nation, and part of the house of Walpole Island First Nation. We recognize and respect all First Nations who have gathered on Pelee Island and remain stewards of the land and waters of Turtle Island.

AT A GLANCE

 GRAND RIVER VALLEY WINERIES
Various locations

 BACKPACKERS SHOP
@thebackpersshop

 APPALACHIAN OUTFITTERS
60 Kendall Park Rd Suite A, Peninsula

 FALLS OUTDOOR COMPANY
1727 Front St, Cuyahoga Falls

 STAR WALK 2
Constellation Star Finder App

 MERLIN
Identify Birds You Hear & See

← *Observatory Park,*
International Dark Sky Park
Daryl Mummey

It was nearly summer, we sat on your roof. Yeah, we smoked cigarettes and we stared at the moon. And I showed you stars you never could see...
Tom Petty

Each August, Earth's orbit passes through debris left by the Swift-Tuttle comet. This debris creates The Perseid Meteor Shower. The Perseids + Observatory Park + Cowboy Camping = One Magical Microadventure.

Every summer during The Perseids, the Geauga Park District lets us camp out for a single night in Montville's Observatory Park. We get to stay up all night watching shooting stars. Sure, you could pitch a tent, but this is an opportunity to Cowboy Camp—just a sleeping bag, bivy sack and nothing else between you and the meteors above.

Observatory Park is Ohio's only certified International Dark Sky Park—lucky for us as urban life across the Western Reserve is littered with ground-light pollution that makes it difficult to see even the Milky Way, one of the bigger galaxies in our universe. And the two observatories, planetarium, on-property hiking trails, and restrooms make dark-sky cowboy camping a short, easy, and achievable microadventure.

Prior to the celestial performance, paddle the Grand River, gravel bike the Red Eagle Loop, MTB Hogback Ridge, SUP Geneva State Park, taste wines at Grand River Valley wineries. Then set up your Cowboy Camp and relax while you wait for the show to begin. Between midnight and dawn you'll see the most shooting stars: sixty to eighty per hour.

Sleeping bag & bivy sack: Backpackers Shop, Appalachian Outfitters, Falls Outdoor Company.

OTHER STUFF

Lean in to astrotourism and download the Star Walk 2 app, an exquisite, free stargazing tool. Year-round Observatory Park is open to gaze at the stars, planets, and galaxies. You can see more when the moon isn't full—but when it is, they offer full-moon hikes. Another annual sight-to-see is at Summit Metro Parks Nimisila Reservoir. Each August, Purple Martins return for an avian performance in the sky some call the *Purple Martins Vortex* (a murmuration). Grab your kayak, SUP, or packraft, paddle into the middle of the reservoir and be an ornithologist for a night. Download the Merlin app.

CLIMB WHIPPS LEDGES

← Jennifer Lynn top-roping Whipps Ledges
Meghan Winkler

I'm a chicken-shit. So, Susan and I just watched the climbers climb. When I was fourteen, I went to a mountaineering school in the San Juan Mountains of Colorado. During my first time roped-in and about to rappel (abseil, controlled descent) a modest rock face, I was surprised to learn I was acrophobic.

For those unafraid of heights, Cleveland Metroparks, local climbing gyms and Ohio Climbers Association are eager to introduce you to their climbing community, climbing ethics, and the sport of top-roping at Whipps Ledges in Cleveland Metroparks Hinckley Reservation.

This microadventure has little in common with documentary films like Alex Honnold's *Free Solo*, Tommy Caldwell's *The Dawn Wall* or Marc-André Leclerc's heartwarming and heartbreaking *The Alpinist*. The urban crag (climbing area) at Whipps Ledges sports thirty-foot sandstone ledges of Sharon Conglomerate, not a 3,000-foot granite monolith like Yosemite's El Capitan.

On par with fly fishing, the learning curve for climbing isn't insignificant but it comes with rich rewards. It quiets the mind as you focus on solving the *problem* (climbing routes are problems that take concentration to figure out). It pays dividends through fitness and self-achievement rewards. And as Rock Mill Climbing Gym puts it—*The community that forms around a shared climb is like no other.* Newcomers often surprise themselves when climbing and bouldering quickly become full-blown hobbies.

Indoor climbing gyms are to Whipps Ledges as Ray's Indoor MTB is to CVNP'S East Rim MTB Trail.

- ☛ Cleveland Rocks
- ☛ Climb Cleveland
- ☛ Kendall Cliffs
- ☛ Nosotros
- ☛ On the Rocks
- ☛ Paddle & Climb
- ☛ Paradisio
- ☛ Rock Mill
- ☛ Shaker Rocks
- ☛ University of Akron

From tourists to microadventuring, Susan and I drove to and hiked nearby Whorden's Ledges (other-worldly carvings.) We road-tripped to Whitey's Booze N' Burgers with an Outside Podcast: "A Bold Rescue on a Moab Cliff" and finished with the Black Keys and Country Maid Ice Cream.

OTHER STUFF

Nearby Hinckley Lake. Rent a Stand Up Paddleboard (SUP) or kayak. In addition to fishing for largemouth bass, based on what an Eagle had in its talons when it flew over my packraft, it looks like Hinkley Lake has rainbow trout, too.

← *Meghan Winkler*

CASTAWAY TO ISLE SAINT GEORGE

AT A GLANCE

GREAT LAKES FLY FISHING
@greatlakesflyfishingllc

LAKE HOUSE
Call (419) 237-2593

GRIFFIN FLYING SERVICE
3255 E State Rd, Port Clinton

DESERT ISLAND DISCS
BBC podcast

← *Dawn patrol on the eastern shore of Isle Saint George to catch the sunrise over Pelee Island*
Gabe Leidy

Remember in *Castaway* when Tom Hanks' character, Chuck Noland, speared his fish? Standing resolutely on that rock, ripped, tan and sportin' those Robert Plant goldilocks, Chuck and father time had slowed waaay down. Without his pager, Fedex countdown clock and mantra that *we live or die by the clock*, Chuck was on *island time*.

There's a nearby desert island where you can slow waaay down: Isle Saint George (aka North Bass Island). It's part of the Bass Islands archipelago, yet no tourist hordes roam this *lost* island. And you can sleep in a house, not a cave.

Start the day on dawn patrol at Honey Point Wildlife Area. Hike, bike, kayak the water trail, ride the ATV, look for LEWS, go birding (shorebirds, songbirds, waterfowl, Northern Bobwhite), hunt for beach glass, grill-out, catnap, skinny-dip. Catch the Holy Trinity (golden hour, sunset, blue hour) on Manilla Bay by Foxs Pond. And without light pollution, the stars and Milky Way Galaxy get a chance to really dazzle.

During May and June fishing guide Jeff Liskay (Great Lakes Fly Fishing) can show up and take you out for a shot at a Lake Erie Grand Slam: catching walleye, freshwater drum and smallmouth bass on the same day.

The hitch? There's no ferry service. No problem. First, call ODNR at (419) 237-2593 and *try* to book the fully-furnished Lake House for a minimum three night stay (sleeps 10–12). Next, you'll need to rent or charter a boat. You can call Griffin Flying Service, but rowdy Lake Erie weather can ground planes and ruin plans—leaving you marooned or unable to get there in the first place. And the boat can bring your bike, kayak, food and blender—*and soon it will render* ...Jimmy Buffet

OTHER STUFF

Listen to the BBC podcast Desert Island Discs for inspiration to curate an Isle Saint George playlist. During final edits, I watched *Castaway* again. *I know what I have to do now. I gotta keep breathing. Because tomorrow the sun will rise. Who knows what the tide could bring.* Chuck Noland.

CATCH A SOLSTICE STEPS SUNSET

AT A GLANCE

 BOOM'S PIZZA
14730 Detroit Ave, Lakewood

 ANGELO'S PIZZA
13715 Madison Ave, Lakewood

 LA PLAZA TAQUERIA
13609 Lakewood Heights Blvd B, Cleveland

 PROPER PIG BBQ
17100 Detroit Ave, Lakewood

 HARLOW'S PIZZA
14319 Madison Ave, Lakewood

 MOMOCHO
1835 Fulton Rd, Cleveland

 DAY OF THE DEAD IN THE USA
Regina Marchi

← *Solstice Steps*
Brian D. Kelly—/@/iamthepod

Jimmy Buffet might have felt a twinge of sadness for us snowbirds—many of whom catch sunsets only on spring breaks in Florida. Yet northern Ohio has countless spots to watch the sky blaze and fade.

One that's in a class all its own is Lakewood Parks Solstice Steps—an installation built expressly so folks can gather together (collective effervescence) on the shores of Lake Erie to watch sunsets and soak in the hues of the golden and blue hours. And it ain't too shabby for full-moon rises. When the moon is full, as you watch the setting sun, turn around—the full moon is rising.

The block-seating steps have been cleverly designed by Akron's Environmental Design Group. Find a spot, curl up your legs, and lean back to watch one of the two greatest natural events that happen every twenty-four hours.

Grab some grub to-go before you get there. Our first time we grabbed some Boom's Pizza. Here's four seasonal sunsets paired with some more Lakewood gems (plus-one):

1. Vernal (spring) equinox with Tom Kess' Angelo's Pizza
2. Summer solstice with Adrian Ortega's La Plaza Taqueria
3. Autumnal (fall) equinox with Shane Vidovic and Ted Dupaski's Proper Pig BBQ
4. Winter solstice and afterwards—due to earlier winter sunsets—Emily Flamos and John Sweeney's Harlow's Pizza
5. Ancestors Day (aka Dia de los Muertos, Day of the Dead) and afterwards, Eric Williams' Ohio City Momocho (smoked trout guac)

At times, Solstice Steps can be carnivalesque, kinda like a muted Mallory Square Sunset Celebration in Key West. For more *stilling* sunsets, try CVNP's Ritchie Ledges Overlook, Indigo Lake, Beaver Marsh, along the pines overlooking Stumpy Basin, or along the fence line at Lake Metroparks Chapin Forest Reservation. On Canada's Pelee Island, the picnic table by the west pump station is a sublime setting. And sunsets from kayaks, SUPs, and packrafts are hard to beat:

☛ Harbor Yak's Sunset Tour, Ashtabula River
☛ 41 North's SUP Set Tour, Rocky River
☛ Nimisila Reservoir—sunset plus Purple Martin Vortex (each August)
☛ LoCo 'Yak's Sunset Tour, Black River
☛ West River Outfitters, Vermillion River
☛ Paddle & Climb, Sandusky Bay

OTHER STUFF

*...some of it's magic, some of it's tragic, but I had a good life all the way...*Jimmy Buffet. Regina Marchi, *Day of the Dead in the USA: The Migration and Transformation of a Cultural Phenomenon.*

PADDLE THE FLATS

AT A GLANCE

 MERWIN'S WHARF
1785 Merwin Ave, Cleveland

 JOHNNY'S LITTLE BAR
614 Frankfort Ave, Cleveland

 @TRASHFISH_CLE

← *The crew at the Salt Mine on the
Old Cuyahoga River channel*
Jeff Suvak

Have you heard any jokes about a Burning River lately? If so, the teller's *cocky ignorance* signals a cluelessness about Earth Day and the Clean Water Act—and that Section five (The Flats) of the Cuyahoga River Water Trail was recently voted USA Today's Number One Best Place in America to Go Paddling in the City.

Paddling The Flats checks all the microadventure boxes when the sun is shining. But as the sun begins to blaze and fade, it's otherworldly. The lights of the City's skyline and the illuminated bridges cast a magical spell as you paddle that fine line between the wilds and urban living on a working river.

It's an urban water trail tailor-made for a paddle in sea kayaks with 41 North Coastal Adventure's Burning River Tour. Put-in and take-out is at Rivergate Park's Merwin's Wharf and its a *downbound* to the Old River Channel. You'll paddle past pleasure boats, ginormous freighters and maybe a tug boat or two. If you're lucky, a sculler or eight-person crew shell might be rowing back to Western Reserve Rowing or The Foundry. You'll paddle under historic lift and swing bridges, past The Flats entertainment district and even towering sand dunes (not a typo). Johnny's Little Bar for the finish. 41 North's Cleveland Rocks Tour is another goodie. Ditto their Lakewood Cliffs and Coves Tour.

Trashfish the Cuyahoga River. Volunteer with Eddie Olschansky (aka Trashfish) to clean up the Cuyahoga one piece of trash at a time. Eddie is a take-no-prisoners kinda guy, out there five days a week fighting the good fight. Eddie will loan you free trash-grabbers and kayaks to help him collect trash before it floats into Lake Erie—the source for drinking water for millions and millions of people.

What kinds of trash? Big plastic tubes, nerdles (not the daily numbers game), styrofoam cups, tires, basketballs, and the occasional sex toy, just to name a few. Another volunteer opportunity is with Canalway Partners and their annual RiverSweep.

OTHER STUFF

Bring your bikes for a post-paddle night ride and Bike the Sokolowski's Loop. Experience the duality of the Cuyahoga River—paddle The Flats and then paddle its sleepy headwaters in Geauga County.

↑ Coppacaw Falls (aka Big Falls)
Courtesy of Peninsula Library

Free the falls →

← *Downtown Sculler*
Matt Shiffler

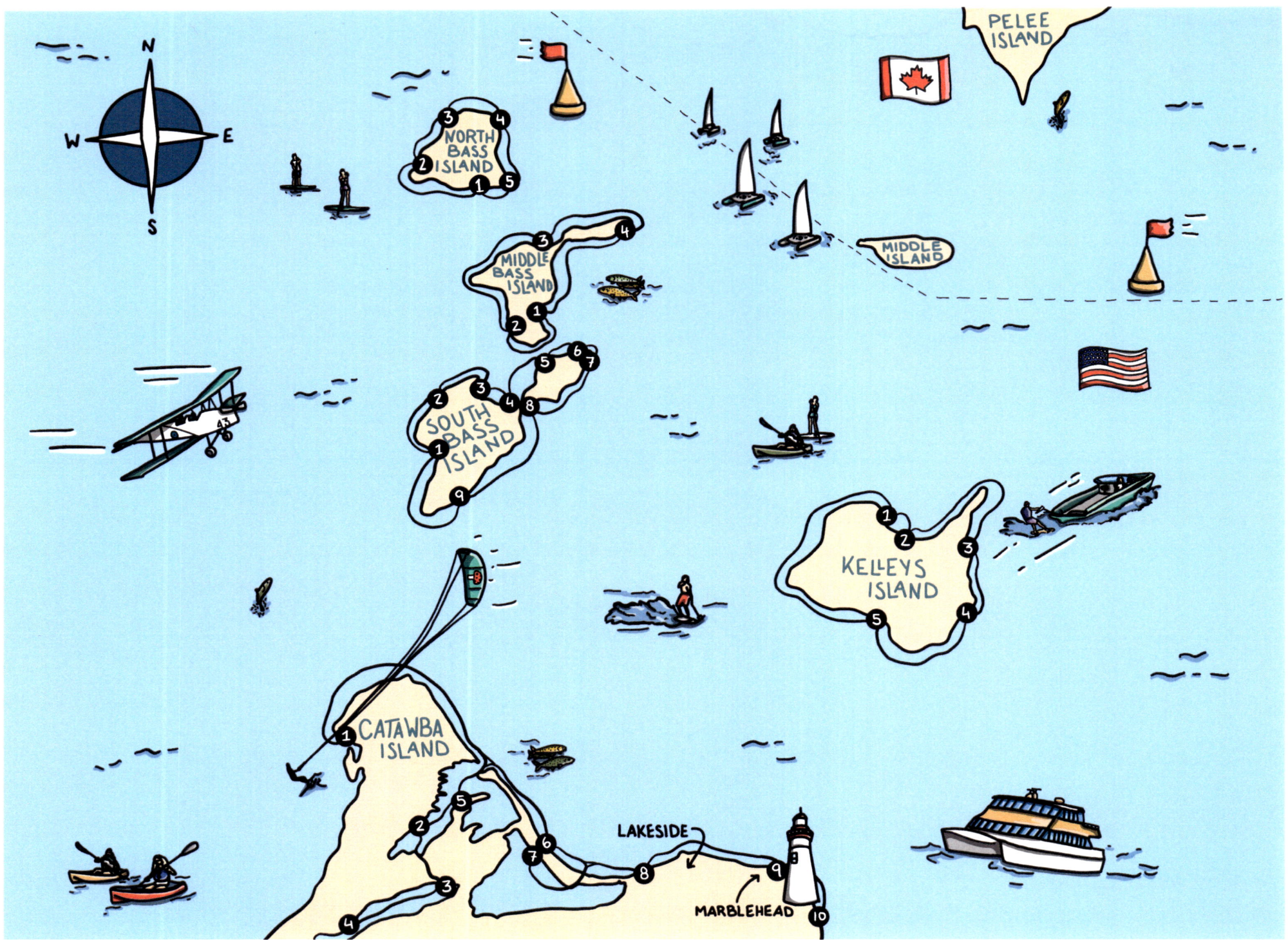

PELEE ISLAND

NORTH BASS ISLAND

MIDDLE BASS ISLAND

MIDDLE ISLAND

SOUTH BASS ISLAND

KELLEYS ISLAND

CATAWBA ISLAND

LAKESIDE

MARBLEHEAD

Sarah Schmitz

PADDLE AN ARCHIPELAGO

AT A GLANCE

 **SOUTH BASS ISLAND
KAYAK RENDEZVOUS**
sbikayayrendezvous.com

← North Bass Island Trail

1. North Bass Island State Park (south)
2. Fox's Marsh Wildlife Area
3. North Bass Island State Park (north)
4. North Bass Island State Park (east)
5. Honey Point Wildlife Area

Middle Bass Island Trail

1. Middle Bass Island Trail (Dock Fee)
2. Middle Bass Island State Park (west)
3. Petersen Woods/Kuehnle Wildlife Area
4. Middle Bass Island East Point Preserve

South Bass Island Trail

1. South Bass Island State Park
2. West Shore Ice Ramp
3. Oak Point State Park
4. Village of Put-in-Bay Public Boat Launch
*   (Dock Fee)*
5. Massie Cliffside Preserve
6. Scheeff East Point Nature Preserve (north)
7. Scheeff East Point Nature Preserve (east)
8. Village of Put-in-Bay Beach
9. Put-in-Bay Port Authority Access

Kelleys Island Trail

1. Kelleys Island State Park
2. North Pond State Nature Preserve
3. Scheele Preserve
4. Woodford Road Access
5. Inscription Rock Petroglyphs

Catawba Island

1. Catawba Island State Park
2. West Harbor Public Boat Launching Ramp
3. Great Egret Marsh Preserve
4. Ottawa National Wildlife Refuge //
*   West Harbor Landing*
5. East Harbor State Park Marina (Launch Fee)
6. East Harbor State Park (Lake Erie)
7. East Harbor State Park (East Harbor)
8. Mazurik Access Area
9. Lucien M. Clemons Park
10. Marblehead Lifesaving Station

Let's say you want to kayak one or all of the water trails on the other page: maybe you've been taught to kayak safely, have your PFD (Personal Flotation Device), checked and double checked the weather forecast, applied your sunscreen, and have your head on a swivel for sailboats, wake boats, and freighters—shit can still go wrong on microadventures that lawyers, guns and money can't fix. Full stop and change of topic.

What's an archipelago? It's a cool sounding name for *a group of islands*. Think of the Hawaiian Islands, that's an archipelago. We have one, too. Along with an array of smaller islands, South Bass Island, Middle Bass Island, North Bass Island (aka Isle Saint George), Kelleys Island (aka Emerald Isle), and Canada's Pelee Island create a group of islands that represent the Lake Erie Islands Archipelago.

When was the last time you did something for the first time?—a clever line from a country song by Darius Rucker. If you're kayak-curious-enough to try something new, you'll have an adventurous answer to that question. Whether you're free soloing or microadventuring with your partner or friends, you'll be able to say:

I did the annual South Bass Island Kayak Rendezvous and paddled that fine line between the wilds and urban living. I rode a ferry, camped, hung out by the campfire, made new friends, paddled all the Lake Erie Islands Water Trails and saw a bunch of sleek racing sailboats. And hell if I didn't paddle out and back to Canada's Pelee Island, too!

Heads Up: Don't show up to the South Bass Island Kayak Rendezvous thinking the organizers are gonna hold your hand, provide you with a sea kayak and teach you what a spray skirt is and how to do a wet exit and self rescue. Sign up for lessons at 41 North Coastal Adventures or Cleveland Metroparks Kayak *Try-It* and *Learn-It* programs. Your local school's pool might offer kayak classes, too.

OTHER STUFF

The Mills Cup race—the premier sailing race in Lake Erie. Held at night and ending at South Bass Island's Put-in-Bay Docks and Marina. It's a cool experience being on the docks when sailboats return to port after a race. And you're in luck, the South Bass Island Kayak Rendezvous is the same weekend as the Mills Cup race. Other Ohio Water Trails: East Sandusky Bay Water Trail, Vermilion-Lorain Water Trail, Lake Erie Water Trail, Cuyahoga River Water Trail.

BACKPACK THE LITTLE LOOP

← *Follow the blue blazes*
Gabe Leidy

The AT (Appalachian Trail) is 2,190 miles long. We have a pretty long trail in Ohio, too. It's called The Buckeye Trail (BT). It's a 1,444-mile trail that loops around our State. Maybe you've seen the two inch by six inch baby blue blazes marking trees—that's the BT.

There's a second, shorter loop within the BT—one that's probably only a few miles from your home. The Buckeye Trail's Little Loop is 250 miles long. It snakes north through Akron, CVNP and up to Mentor Headlands and Lake Erie, then loops back south through Chardon, Burton, Hartville, and Canal Fulton. The Little Loop trail takes you through six park districts, each offering some type of camping (hiking + camping = backpacking). A big thanks to Rachel and Ashley from Cleveland Metroparks who guided me to this backpacking microadventure.

If you haven't done much hiking and have little-to-no backpacking experience, the Little Loop is a solid place to start, practice and build confidence. (Night hike it, too).

Since it's so close to home, a single night under the stars offers first-timers a less stressful way to try camping—both tent and cowboy camping. Gear up at Backpackers Shop, Appalachian Outfitters, Falls Outdoor Company.

While backpacking the AT might be a once in a lifetime experience, hiking the BT's Little Loop can be a first in a lifetime of experiences. Some folks hike the Little Loop over a number of years.

Others *complete* the 250-mile trail in a single day by participating in the Little Loop Challenge and hiking it collectively. Little Loop is divided into seventy-seven segments ranging from half a mile to six and a half miles. Hike whatever distance you want. Check out buckeyetrail.org for more info plus opportunities to volunteer.

OTHER STUFF

Three-day backpack trip. Hike from Cleveland Metroparks Bedford Reservation to camp at Brecksville Reservation's Ottawa Overlook Backcountry site. Day two, hike to the Inn at Brandywine Falls and rest your weary bones in a bed. Day three, ride CVSR to Botzum Station or Northside Station and hike the Towpath, Valley Bridle and Buckeye trails north for a final night camping under the stars at Christmas Tree Farm or Valley Overlook at Camp Mueller.

BUCKEYE TRAIL

BIKEPACK YOUR HOME TURF

AT A GLANCE

 SILVER SPRINGS CAMPGROUND
5238 Young Rd, Stow

 HERITAGE FARM
6050 Riverview Rd, Peninsula

 VALLEY OVERLOOK
4451 Akron Peninsula Rd, Peninsula

 CLEVELAND.COM
John Pana's outdoor videos

 BIKEPACKING.COM
Biking Resource

 INN AT BRANDYWINE FALLS
8230 Brandywine Rd, Northfield

 LARDER DELI
1455 W 29th St, Cleveland

 DIAMOND DELI
378 S Main St, Akron

 LORDS OF THE FLY
Monte Burke

 A PASSION FOR TARPON
Andy Mill

 ← *Illustration inspired
by bikepacking.com
Sarah Schmitz*

My bicycle touring days are probably over. After graduating from the University of Akron, I rode and camped my baby-blue Schwinn Continental 1,400 miles from Richmond, Virginia to Boca Grande Florida—which some consider the tarpon capital of the world (Capt Babe Darna helped me and my dad catch our first).

I'm grateful for the experience but those back-to-back 100+ mile days, getting run down by a frothy-mouthed Georgia pitbull and too many close calls with cars and one jacked-up, puke-green, F-250 pickup truck...well, enough is enough.

Bikepacking northern Ohio, however, is a horse of a different color: while it's a multi-day bike trip, thanks to our robust network of bike trails, bikepacking here at home is almost an entirely off-road affair—so no jacked-up, puke-green F-250 pickup trucks.

Cleveland Metroparks Emerald Necklace (Valley Parkway All-Purpose trails) and the Towpath Trail connect to one another at Brecksville Reservation. And thanks to the The Bike & Hike / Towpath Connector Trail (aka Old Carriage Trail), the Towpath connects to Summit Metro Parks Bike & Hike Trail. These connections create ample route configurations. Add-in the camping component with Silver Springs Campground, Christmas Tree Farm (aka Heritage Farms) and Valley Overlook at Camp Mueller and you can bikepack the hell out of your home turf.

This microadventure is bikepacking-lite, however. We'll skip the camping—which eliminates most of the gear pictured on the opposite page. Photo courtesy of bikepacking.com—a Library of Congress-worthy resource for outdoor adventures by bike.

Basecamp: Inn at Brandywine Falls. Two nights in their big, comfy Loft bed and two mornings with their Greta Garbo *I want to be alone* breakfast service.
Day One: Bike the Towpath and Emerald Necklace loop (lunch at Cleveland's Hingetown neighborhood gem, Larder Deli).
Day Two: Bike Summit Bike & Hike trail to Summit Freedom trail to Towpath trail and back to the Inn at Brandywine Falls (lunch at Akron's Diamond Deli).

OTHER STUFF

GOBA—Great Ohio Bike Adventure. Michael and I rode this for our father-son, tenth-birthday adventure. It's bikepacking-lite. GOBA tractor-trailers truck your gear from Gobaville to Gobaville, they have mobile showers and I've never seen a single puke-green F-250 pickup truck. Speaking of tarpon: Monte Burke's *Lords of the Fly* and Andy Mills' *A Passion for Tarpon.*

BSAG THE LEDGES

I ran away to Rhode Island because of a Chrissie Hynde song and Talking Heads concert at Blossom Music Center. That's a story for another time—I'm just using that as a set up to introduce my sister Annie. She and I saw Talking Heads *Stop Making Sense* tour together.

Annie and I do something we call the *BSAG*—the Brother-Sister Annual Getaway. It began when I got married and it's become an annual ritual to tend to the brother-sister relationship. Like *Fight Club*, we have some rules:

It's just the two of us. Unless it's an emergency, no calls or texts to or from home. The BSAG starts Thursday and ends on Monday (no Sunday travel). And the BSAG has to take place near a body of water like the Outer Banks or Lake Michigan.

Due to the *cocky ignorance* I wrote about in the Boiling Frog story, historically Annie and I had never considered doing a BSAG in northern Ohio, not once. But that's changed and what follows is the itinerary for the next BSAG, with some microadventures shortened to make it all fit.

Thursday night we'll stay in Akron at Tony Troppe's BLU-Tique Hotel or the Courtyard by Marriott (Northside Speakeasy).

Friday night we'll sleep at home and watch *The Blair Witch Project*.

Saturday night we'll stay in Tremont at Fat Cats Chef/Owner Ricardo Sandoval's bistro apartment (Airbnb) or Kimpton Schofield Hotel. Watch Terri Garr (Lakewood) in *Young Frankenstein*.

Sunday night we'll sleep at home and watch the remastered *Stop Making Sense* movie.

BSAG Nano-Microadventures
☛ Ride the Rails, Bike the Trail
☛ Ride the Rails, Paddle the River
☛ Creek-Walk Furnace Run at Everett Covered Bridge (pick up some corn from Szalay's, visit Deep Lock Quarry)

BSAG Microadventures
☛ Bike the Sokolowski's Loop
☛ Hike Brandywine Gorge Trail (then drive to Mitchell's Ice Cream at the Boston Store followed by a visit to CVNP's visitor center to see the Cuyahoga River Valley mural)
☛ MTB the Royalview trail at Mill Stream Run Reservation
☛ Hike the Ledges Trail via Happy Days Lodge/Haskell Run and catch a sunset at the Overlook
☛ Hike Summit Metro Parks Liberty Park Ledges Trail (afterwards, a reflexology session at RG Foot Spa)

BSAG Breakfasts: Mustard Seed Cafe, Blue Door Café (quickies to Summit Metro Parks Overlook Trail, Signal Tree and Don Drumm sculpture) and Martha On The Fly. If we had more time while we were in Cleveland, The Judith (Sardine & Rouille), Le Petit Triangle and Karen Small's Juneberry Table.

BSAG Lunches: Swensons, Larder Deli, Dave's Cosmic Subs (Stretchlab session.)

BSAG Dinners: Luigi's, raw shucked oysters at Downtown 140 followed by smashburgers at The Farmer's Rail—and while we're overnighting in Cleveland, depending on Annie's mood, Fat Cats, Il Rione, Momocho, Mabel's BBQ, SoHo Chicken + Whiskey, LJ Shanghai, Zhug, Cordelia or Goma—all the while keeping an eagle eye out for new Doug Trattner restaurant reviews and ears tuned for new Lisa Sands' CLE Foodcast Podcasts.

Sunday we'll have dinner at home: Joe's BBQ plus sides and Szalay's sweet corn (and finish it all off with a couple oatmeal creme pies from Larder Deli that we picked up on Saturday while we were there for lunch—fried chicken sammich for Annie, Koji-cured pastrami sammich for me and potato salad for both).

On Monday, after breakfast at Fred's Diner, Annie will fly out of Akron-Canton back to Chicago.

For The Record. We'll listen to music from our "Yutes": Peter Tosh's Wanted Dread or Alive, heroic doses of Grateful Dead, English Beat, Bob Marley, New Order, Roxy Music's Avalon album, Toots & The Maytals, Chrissie Hynde and Pretenders, Bob Dylan's Desire album, Alex Bevan's Skinny, songs from that anniversary video we made for mom and dad from those 9mm home movies—songs like Randy Travis' "Forever and Ever", and "Deeper Than the Holler", The Judds' "Why Not Me" and "Grandpa" and Neil Young's "Comes a Time"—and all the other music we had on those mix-tapes we made together. Love you, kiddo.

← Ritchie Ledges—Ledges Overlook
Nick Hoeller

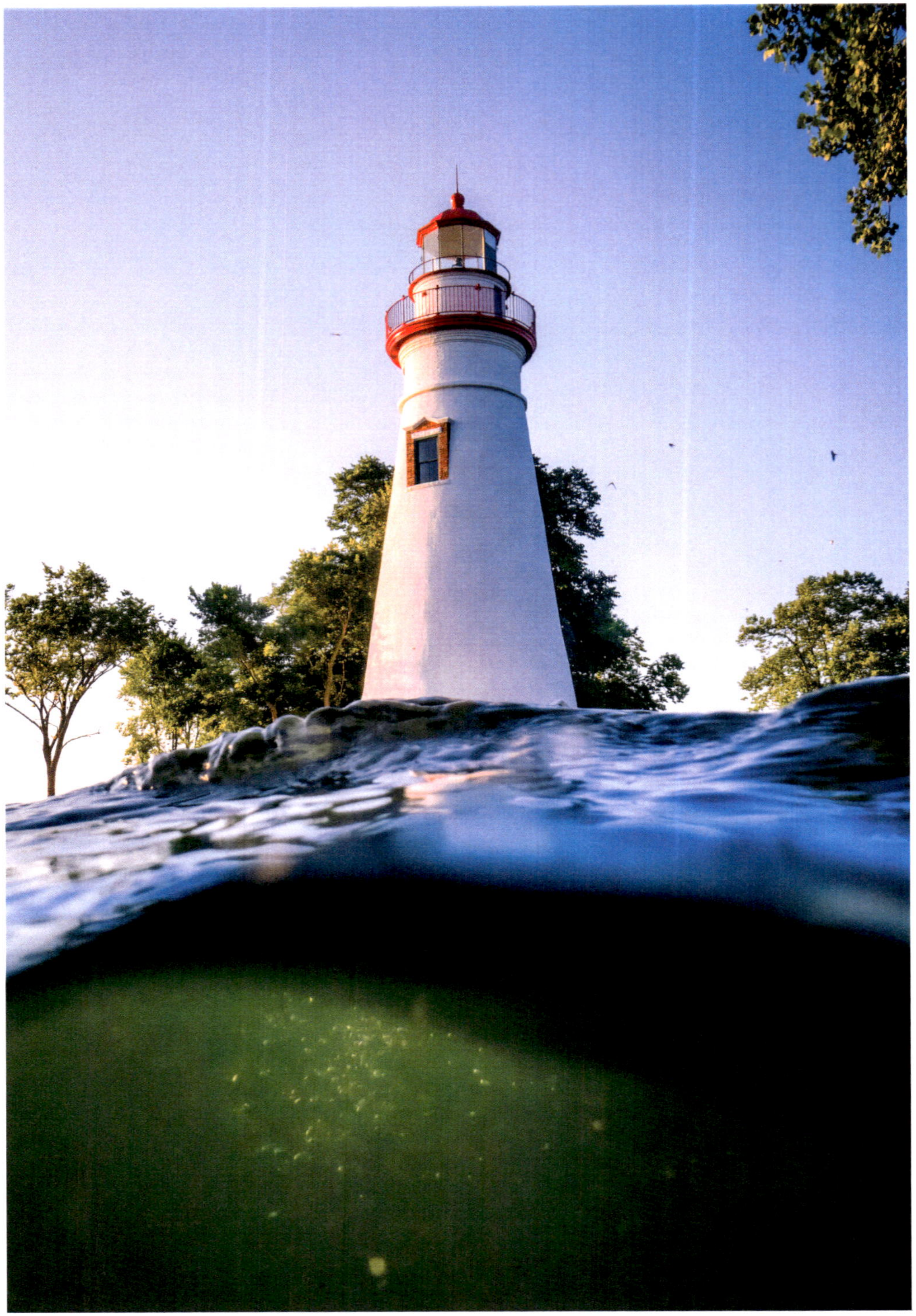

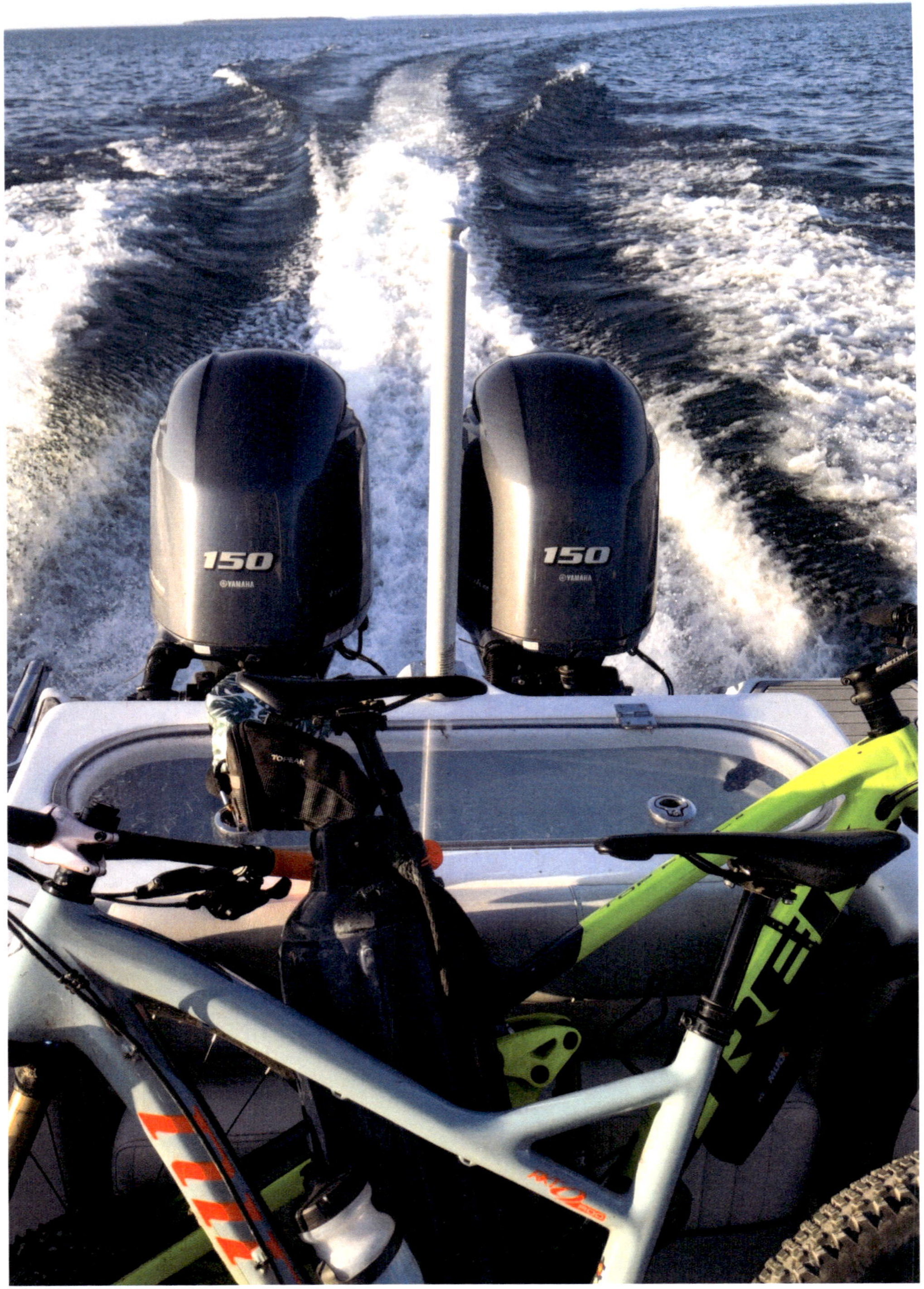
150
150

FAT BIKE LAKE ERIE'S EMERALD ISLE

Full Disclosure: I haven't done this microadventure... yet. But I have a gameplan thanks to Bret Maiers and Ryan *Otis* Adams, the founder and owner of Akron's Dirty River Bicycle Works (across the street from Luigi's Pizza). You might remember Otis guided me and my gravel bike to the "Gravel Bike Mitchell's Ice Cream Loop" microadventure.

Ryan connected me to Bret, an islander, the owner of the Caddy Shack Restaurant and Bar and the Island House Restaurant—and a mountain biker. This microadventure is made possible because of Bret's MTB stoke: he's a co-founder of Kelleys Island Trail and Bike Association. KITABA is a 501(c)(3) dedicated to promoting, maintaining, building and improving trails on Kelleys Island (KI). KI is also known as Lake Erie's *Emerald Isle*.

Yes, there are MTB trails on KI, trails which Otis characterizes as *amazing and light difficulty*. This sets the stage for a long-weekend microadventure that will also include the Marblehead Lighthouse and South and Middle Bass Islands. And with my *ferry thing*, I'm jazzed that this microadventure includes six ferry rides. (Seven if you take the water taxi to Gibraltar Island.)

Seeing as I haven't done this microadventure yet, the 411 on this one is slim pickens; basically I've mapped out the logistics and once I'm on island, I'll wing it from there.

These days I'm not keen to camp but Otis had big praise for the campsites at Kelleys Island State Park (super-close to the Glacial Grooves and Lake Erie). As far as accommodations, my friend Peg (a summer islander) suggested I investigate places to stay via Airbnb and StayonKI.com. She also shared that the Kelleys Island Facebook group is super-helpful, too.

Sidebar on Peg: along with Katie and Diana, Peg was one of the angels who coordinated and arranged all the beautiful flowers for Cooper's Cleveland COL. And Peg and her husband say Bret's Island House Restaurant is their fave restaurant. I'm looking forward to trying one particular beer at Bret's place: Findlay Brewing's *Brilliant Blonde Ale*.

A *few* words on Fat Bikes:

☛ I don't have a Fat Bike, but I wish I did. My friend Jay loaned me his and with its massive, 3.7 to 5.2 inch tires to maintain massive contact with the ground, fat bikes can *float* over damn near anything

☛ If I consider gravel bikes to be adventure bikes (and I do), then fat bikes are uber-adventure bikes with their cushy ride and ability to maintain traction in areas with unforgiving terrain like snow and mud—and sandy KI, South Bass and Middle Bass Island beaches

☛ Bottom line: fat bikes are absurdly fun bikes to ride

Three different ferries, six ferry rides:

☛ For starters, I'll catch the Kelleys Island Ferry out of mainland Marblehead to KI. I'll ferry over with my vehicle and electric mountain bike (eMTB)

☛ As this is a long-weekend microadventure, I've got a day-trip excursion planned off KI: my bike and I will catch the Jet Express Ferry from KI to Put-in-Bay on South Bass Island. I'll explore the island by bike

☛ Then I'll take the Sonny S Inter-Island Ferry from South Bass to Middle Bass Island and do the same thing there: explore the island by bike

☛ That adds up to four ferry rides in one day by the time I return to KI—add in the out-n-back on the Kelleys Island Ferry and that makes six ferry rides in one microadventure

OTHER STUFF

Dial up some Pat *The Coolest SOB in The World* Daily on Spotify—and Google him, too: together Pat and Put-in-Bay make for an interesting story. When there's snow on the ground, fat bike Punderson State Park's groomed cross-country ski and snowmobile trails.

(L) Marblehead Lighthouse
Gabe Leidy

(R) Bike-by-Boat island-hopping: Twin-engine run from USA's Kelley's Island to Canada's Pelee Island.
Bret Maiers

So I say, ready or not
Yeah, here comes the funeral.
"Ready or Not," Shakey Graves, Sierra Ferrell

A widow, solo mom, writer and grief counselor I follow on Instagram has a post about the death of her partner that lands with me:

It's one of the first things I thought when he died and its continued to be THE HARDEST thing about this:

He's dead and he's never coming back.
Period. Full stop.
There is no ending to this.
Mira Simone

Sidebar: widow, widower, orphan. What's the word for a mother whose child has died?

The five-stages of grief model, developed by Elisabeth Kübler-Ross, became famous after she published her book *On Death and Dying* in 1969. Kübler-Ross developed her framework to describe people with a terminal illness facing their own death. But soon it was conflated as a way of thinking about grief and grieving in general. Kübler-Ross didn't develop her five-stages of grief to describe what people go through when a loved one dies.

Yet well-meaning people incorrectly took it to mean that grieving follows a linear process—where the bereaved steadily move through each progressive stage in a tidy and timely fashion, eventually coming out the other side with closure, whole again, back to normal, all better, all good—grief gone.

Cooper's death isn't about *closure* for me. In my brief relationship with sudden, unexpected and traumatic loss, grief doesn't go away, it doesn't disappear—and in my way of thinking, it shouldn't.

Speaking only for myself—and quoting author, philosopher Stephen Jenkinson (discovered via Cooper)—*grief is a way of loving that which has slipped from view...* Framed another way, did my love for Coop die the night he died? *Forget it, Donny. You're out of your element.* So, why in the wide wide world of sports would I ever think or expect or wish for my grief to go away?

My heart is broken and I never want it to heal. I want only for it to get bigger. Period. Full stop. *Befriending* my grief, coming into relationship with it and not treating it like an unwelcome guest might be an opportunity for my broken heart to stay open and embrace another piece of Jenkinson wisdom that *grief is the midwife of your capacity to be immensely grateful for being born.* But don't let me fool you; I don't have this shit-show figured out. I'm trusting in a process—a process of learning to do the grief work.

While the stakes are higher, as I wade into this unfamiliar territory as an adult-beginner, learning to tend to the grief is not unlike fishing guide Jeff Liskay describing learning to fly fish: fly fishing presents a learning curve that requires dedication, but it comes with big self-achievement rewards and it's damn good for the soul. I'm not so sure about the *big self-achievement rewards* but I do know that learning about grief and grieving has been damn good for my soul.

On the subject of microadventures, how does nature work its magic on us? Does it have something to do with the Scandinavian practice of Friluftsliv (open-air life) or *your brain on nature* and the inverse relationship between blood cortisol levels and coherence in the alpha or gamma frequencies? I have no fucking clue; I'm fine leaving the source of nature's magic medicine with the mysteries.

← Speaking of American Buffalo, Red Run Bison Farm, Marshallville

Some days, though, traveling through nature on foot, on a mountain bike, in packrafts fishing with Socrates or soaring over it all in a sailplane are no match for the grief. A session with Sarah the death doula isn't enough. A session with Dana the medium isn't enough. Re-reading grief books isn't enough. Listening to grief podcasts isn't enough. Distracting myself with *Shoresy* and @old.time.hawkey reels isn't enough. Some days I need a different medicine: I need to take my grief, the unbearableness, into ritual. Ready or not, some days are buffalo days.

These are the days when my grief is just too heavy and dense, it's energy too wild and feral—and no matter what's on the calendar, I can't get out of bed. On days like these, I borrow something from the American Buffalo: when a storm is approaching, they don't turn tail and run from it, they turn to face the storm—and walk towards it. On days when I can't get out of bed, I lean into the grief with music that reminds me of Coop.

Music we played at his wake, his cremation ceremony, his sacred pipe ceremony, his Celebration of Life ceremonies in Vancouver and Cleveland and his ash ceremony in Michigan—and favorite songs, now lamentations, on a Spotify playlist I've named "Buffalo Days".

My ritual intention is to amplify the grief, to make the misery a little more difficult to bear—so I cry more. A good cry *rinses* me out. More tears move more castings of my grief—the hucha—up and out of my system; I gotta make room for more as there is no ending to this.

There's no English word for the grief I feel when I'm ambushed by the excruciating presence of Cooper's absence in my life (it's wild to be ambushed by something I already know to be true). A Welsh word is *hiraeth* and in the Portuguese culture it's *saudade*—but even their ancient words struggle, and ultimately fail, to convey the ineffable.

And I can't describe the *anemoia*—an ache borne out of the shattered assumptions of his death—a sorrowful, cruel nostalgia for times never known: no wedding for Coop and Mackenzie, no babies, no more conversations and hugs with his mom, no first Steelhead with Socrates and his dad, no more late nights at West Bay with his brothers Henry, Michael, and Maxwell—and countless more secondary losses.

An element of this grief ritual thing is not unlike the liminal state between the eddy turn and eddy peel out found in whitewater kayaking and packrafting; or the transitional period between dark sky and first luminous light of dawn, or the faded moments among a sunset's holy trinity, or a ferry ride from mainland to island. This buffalo day ritual is a *stilling thing*—a stilling thing that seems to get the grief unstuck (and me out of bed).

Before I close the ritual, I acknowledge that our family isn't the only family whose person died: sixty-seven million other souls found 2022 to be their last year among us.

While I'm dumbfounded by it—given my new loyal companion, my ride or die, my *melancholic echo* as Francis Weller calls it—I close by giving thanks for my expanding *capacity to be immensely grateful for being born*. Ready or not, some days are buffalo days.

OTHER STUFF
Red Run Bison Farm, Marshallville. They sell their buffalo meat Saturdays 9 am to noon at CVNP's Farmer's Market At Howe Meadow when it's warm, and when it's frosty, at Old Trail School (love you, Coop Doggy Dawg's babysitter). Buffalo meat is low in fat, slightly sweet and juicy—just don't overcook it. *American Buffalo: In Search of a Lost Icon*, by Steven Rinella. *The American Buffalo*, a film by Ken Burns. *The Rise of Theodore Roosevelt*, by Edmund Morris. *The Mysteries* by Bill Watterson. Keep an eye out for Archipelago Films' (Andy Young & my cousin Susan Todd) new documentary, *HARDWIRED*. It explores how nature works its magic on us. Archipelagofilms.com

↑ *Dawn Patrol, CVNP's Indigo Lake | Gabe Leidy*

SOAR THE WESTERN RESERVE

As a life-long acrophobic, my palms were damp even before Mike from The Cleveland Soaring Society asked his BIG question: *When we're up there, a mile-high over northern Ohio, gliding in the sailplane, do you want A: a nice, smooth ride or do you want B: the "Matterhorn" ride—with stalls and wing-overs and big rides on big thermals?*

I was sweating bullets when I pulled into the Geauga County Airport. After Coop died, I'd adopted a practice of saying a prayer and supercharging it with tobacco in times just like these. Minutes later, I got a silent call from Cooperstown, NY and after I sent a screen capture to Team 5, Mackenzie saw the validation sign I'd missed: the call came in at 5:07. Cooper died May 7th.

Turns out Matterhorn Mike is afraid of heights, too. But for some reason, up there in the sailplane, even when doing stalls and wing-overs and riding big thermals, no fear for either of us. At some point Matterhorn Mike asked if I wanted to take the stick and fly for a bit, but I rainchecked—I was busy.

Busy looking around and remembering. Remembering days way down there, days that I could only really see from way up here. I imagined my own vista-with-text version of Stephen Hannock's *Cuyahoga Dawn*—chock full of love, happy times and microadventures with Susan and my friends—and all of it underscored by the excruciating presence of Cooper's absence in my life.

The hucha hikes with Susan. The first pair of Steelhead Socrates and I ever caught. Bobby taking me on my first MTB ride. Jay lending me his eMTB for the summer. MTB rides with AJ and Stefan at CVNP's Lamb Loop trail. The splendid solitude on solo MTB rides at Summit Metro Parks, Bedford and Mill Stream Run Reservations. Being kidnapped by Socrates, Stefan and AJ and catching my first largemouth bass at AJ's parent's backyard pond.

Gravel bike rides with Scott and Mighty Joe. Grief walks with Wayne, Heidi, Diana and Abby. Flying a huge-ass *heavy lifter show kite* with Drob at Barlow Park. The Cleveland Orvis Fly Fishing classes with Diane and Scott—where I sensed for the first time the magic and mystery and healing disabled active military service personnel say they feel when fly fishing with Project Healing Waters. Leslie introducing Susan and me to the big world of birding during the annual Great Backyard Bird Count. The countless packrafting trips on rivers, lakes and ponds to fish with Socrates.

And then the sailplane caught a thermal, the lift pulling us higher and higher and Canada and the dedication of Cooper's *Pride Rock* at The Hill Academy came into view. I remembered Coop's lacrosse coaches Brodie and Peter Merrill spontaneously confessing the most comforting condolences Susan and I had ever heard: *This is really shitty.*

Dave Eggers, in his wonderful tale *The Eyes & The Impossible* that I read on Pelee Island at The Wandering Dog Inn, illustrates that *comfort* beautifully through a conversation between the one-eyed squirrel, Sonja, and the dog, Johanness.

It's a nasty thing, she said. *Nasty and brutish.*

I had never heard her so passionate. Her anger made me feel good. I can't explain it. It's like she took the fire inside me, put it in a torch, and then set it between us. It was no longer just mine.

On another thermal, I remembered another day in Canada. A day when Susan and I took a hike in Vancouver's Pacific Spirit Park—just days after Cooper's Cremation Ceremony. We were with Cooper's friend Cole and a bereaved dad whose son had been killed three years earlier while trying to save two friends who'd been washed over a waterfall.

With tears of grief streaming down his cheeks, Brad declared that *with no regret, no guilt, and no shame, I can say that after years of grief work, I am living a life more full of love, empathy, compassion, wonder, awe, curiosity and joy than before Ryker's death. And where has all that beauty and gratitude I've found in loss and grief come from? I've learned it all from my son.*

← (L) A mile-high with Matterhorn Mike

(R) The Schweizer SGS 2-32, an American two-seat, mid-wing glider

COOPER KNIGHT CHARLTON   1993 - 2022
TAKE A BREATH, SING A SONG, SAY A PRAYER
WHAT ARE YOU BEING IN THE DOING?

EPILOGUE

2024 marks the fifty-fourth year I've lived three miles from the Cuyahoga River Valley, the Big Five-Oh for Cuyahoga Valley National Park and seven years microadventuring northern Ohio. It also marks twenty-nine years since hometown cartoonist, Bill Watterson, drew the last panels of his comic strip, Calvin and Hobbes.

With each brand new day, Bill's daily strip made us feel more and more connected to Calvin, the adventurous six year-old boy and Hobbes, his sardonic stuffed tiger.

Essentially Cuyahoga Valley Microadventures is a story about a boy and his friends and the adventures they went on together—including the experience of Cooper's death at age twenty-nine.

If I knew how to reach Bill, I'd ask permission to use his last strip when Calvin and Hobbes went sledding. With tender-hearted poignancy, it says everything I want to say about microadventures—and practicing the wisdom that *grief is the midwife of your capacity to be immensely grateful for being born.*

Everything familiar has disappeared.

There's treasure everywhere.

It's like having a big white sheet of paper to draw on. A day full of possibilities.

It's a magical world, Hobbes, ol' buddy.

Let's go exploring!

If I could, I'd draw into Bill's last strip something that evokes a delicate but potent personal revelation from the Cooper Charlton Spiritual Summer School. It's inscribed on his bench at Jericho Beach in Vancouver—the spot where Cooper asked Mackenzie to marry him:

What are you being in the doing?

My wish here at the end is the same as my wish at the beginning: that the energy I've put into this project might serve to help someone in some way some day—and on that day, may you find parts of yourself you didn't know were there.

← *Cooper's Bench*
Cole Nakatani

KICKSTARTER UPDATE #18

Ok.

That's it.

I'm callin' it.

With the exception of one lone backer who's outta town in her happy place—Sarah (Coop's babysitter)—everyone who backed the book on Kickstarter got their book, right?!

Right.

Susan, AJ and I hand-delivered or mailed 120 books to 120 backers—from Vancouver, Denver and Chicago, to Toronto, Ann Arbor and Pelee Island. From Akron, Hudson and Cleveland, to Annapolis, Mattapoisett and Katy in Paris, France.

And the three of us hand-delivered the remaining 100 copies as Thank You gifts to the beauties who contributed photos and art to the book—as well as inspirational folks mentioned and pictured on its pages.

So I'm callin' it: this'll be the last Kickstarter update you'll get from me, and that'll be all she wrote on this chapter of the CVMA book. Now it's cards-on-the-table time—or as they say, *don't bore us, get to the chorus.*

Time to pull back the curtain on why I've often written in Kickstarter updates *I'm grateful for you backers*—and inscribed many of your signed books with the same. Some backers guessed it was a trippy nod to being a Grateful Dead superfan; not quite.

My gratitude exists because you gifted me a purpose. In a time when beauty and meaning were hard to find, you gave me a purpose to go find both.

When you backed the book, it was a far cry from publication-ready: I had eight more microadventure stories to write, a shedload of photos to curate and a slew of art to commission. A daunting project for a dad whose world was ruptured by the amputation of his son's sudden, unexpected and traumatic out-of-order death.

So what's an untethered writer to do? I created a village-making event with the Kickstarter campaign—and you showed up and backed the book. Now I was on-the-hook. I had a promise to keep. A commitment to honour. A mission to complete and a deadline to meet.

While I could say you became my *silent partners,* it would be more accurate to describe you as the *dissertation committee* waiting on my Capstone Project from the Cooper Charlton Spiritual Summer School. *The purpose of a capstone project is to challenge students to think critically, solve problems, and demonstrate the student's readiness for their field of work.*

I came to see the writing I did after Cooper's death as a way of demonstrating to myself a *readiness* to carry what can't be fixed, to do the grief work, to live a life without one of my children. Irish novelist Samuel Beckett hit this intention on the head with *I can't go on, I'll go on* (no *buts* about it).

Sarah the death doula talks about a *Blessed Catastrophe*. The hard part of death (catastrophe) just happens. The blessing was something I had to make. Sarah taught me that if I met Cooper's death with the intention of bringing beauty and meaning to it, the blessings found could be profound. Civilian hint: the blessings don't cancel out the grief.

We shake with joy, we shake with grief.
What a time they have, these two,
housed as they are in the same body.
Mary Oliver

And the writing offered me a chance to wonder about some things; and born of that wonder, some reckonings: as I'll cry til I die, how will I ever be happy again? Why do things happen like they do? Why does it matter that I'm alive? What's the meaning and direction of my life? What happens to us when we die?

Know this: you did a blessed thing for an unmoored dad. You bound me to an odyssey—a long wandering to find buried treasures (blessings) while writing microadventure stories where Cooper and grief showed up. You tossed me a lifeline. It wouldn't be too big a stretch to see yourself as *Clarence*—and me as *George Bailey*—in the classic *It's a Wonderful Life*.

Ok. That's it. I'm callin' it—and ending with a little Ram Dass (one of Coop's faves):

We're all just holding hands and walking each other home.

Thanks for holding mine.

All My Relations, David
September 17, 2024

Chiaroscuro →
Matt Greene

BACKERS

Charlie Adams
The Adams Family
Atchison Family
Ator Family
Heidi Augustin
Susana Banks
Diana Berrow
Hayden Bitler
Bunn
Jess PB
Jennie Campbell Peterson
Scott Campbell
McCormick Chan
David A Charlton Family
Michael Charlton
Chris Colby Family
Captain Cooke
Emily "Free Range" Cordonnier
Katie Coulton
Nicholas Custer
Rebecca Drohan Cravens
Adam Dunne
Ellie Fabe & Frank Russell
Ellie Falzone
Joe Fiedler
Parke FitzGerald & Family

Stefan Gaspar
Joe Graf
Matthew Greene
Kelsey Greissing
Griff Hill Family
Leah Gripp
The Gripp Girls
Guadagni Family
The Hancsak Family
Lori Hart
Tom & Kristen Haydock
Kevin & Abby Hellman
Mackenzie Henry
MB & Tom Henry
Leigh Ann Hetsler
Michael Hogan
Zach Hruby
Doug, Amy, Cooper & Gil Kaplan
The Kerch Family
Kaitlyn Kincannon
Sam & Kristen Kline
Kate Krum
Di & John
Jason & Jeri Levand
Liotta Johnston Family
Lockwood Family

Jake & Anna Love
Marylee & Brad Maendler
Mia Maendler
Trent Maendler
Leslie Mapes
Melissa Mather
Peg & Tom Mayor
Becky Montgomery Tucker
Connor Morris
Morrison Family
Morrison Family
Mick, Scott & Peter Mougey
Linda Mudler
Wendell Mueller
Charlie Murphy
Joe Murphy
Tom & Lisa Murphy
Tyler Peacock
Mallory & Henry Perazzo
Rhein Family
Brendan Riefberg & Kelsey Greissing
Rittinger/Katz
Julie, David, Reid & Jena Robinson
Schroeder Family
AJ Sekerak
Hannah Sekerak & Jonathan Fruth

Michael & Ann Sekerak
Nate Shaw
The Shaw Family
Stephanie Stanziano
Angela Strach-Gotthardt
Paul Studer
Salli Swindell
Brian & Diana Taussig
Diana Taussig
The Thomas Family
Tom Tobin Family
Andrew Todd Family
Michael Todd Family
Adam Tucker Family
Carol Turner
Charlie Urbancic
Rachel Van Voorhis
Andy VandenBerg Family
Sarah Waitkus
Barb & Jeff Warner
Paige Warner
The Warner Family
Wayne Wallace Family
Abby Weary Wenstrup
Whitt & Acosta Family
Matt Withem

CONTRIBUTORS

HEIDI AUGUSTIN

DEREK DEYOUNG
Web—derekdeyoung.com
IG—derek.deyoung
FB—deyoung.studio

JOSEPH FIEDLER
Web—joefiedler.com
IG—joefiedler

MATT GREENE
Web—kindportraits.com
Email—matthew@matthewgreenephotography.com

RYAN GRZYBOWSKI
Web—ryansfotos.com

ERIC HANCSAK
Web—about350.com

STEPHEN HANNOCK (L)
Web—stephenhannock.com
IG—stephenhannock

NICK HOELLER
Web—hoellerphotography.com

KIM KARBON
IG—*@scenebyme_cle*
Facebook—*Kim Karbon Photography*

YEHYUN LEE
Drawing IG—*h.y.u.n.2*
Personal IG—*yehyunliz*
Web—*yehyunlee.com*

GABE LEIDY
Business—*Gabe Leidy Photography*

JULIE ROBINSON

SARAH SCHMITZ
IG—*sarahwait_*
Email—*indicaillustrations@gmail.com*

MATT SHIFFLER
Web—*mattshifflerphotography.com*

IAN VIRTUE
Web—*ianvirtue.com*
IG—*ian.virtue*

MEGHAN WINKLER
Web—*meghanwinkler.com*

COLLABORATORS

EMILY CORDONNIER
IG—em_co_design
Email—emilymarie.cordonnier@gmail.com

AJ SEKERAK
IG—aj_sek
Email—ajsekerak@gmail.com

Maybe it was written in the stars, but in 2017 when David was forming the idea for this book, there was a girl in a small Ohio town dreaming of all the adventures to come in life. That year I wrote and gave my high school valedictorian speech about how *adventure is out there* and I guess I found it. As a native Ohioan I've always had a fascination of the hidden gems this state has to offer. Growing up one of my favorite books was (and still is) *Weird Ohio*, it has captivated me to traverse this place I call home. One day I will find the strange Kirtland Melon heads or elusive Loveland Frogman. This project spoke to me on a love for this place, but also as someone who holds almost a decade of grief after losing a childhood friend too soon. I take her joyous lust for life in every adventure. So to call this project *near and dear to my heart* is an understatement. *Grief is love with everywhere to go.*

Prior to meeting David, my love for Northern Ohio was already established and deeply intertwined with my day to day life. A pack of fresh strawberries from Szalay's and the warmth of a Richie's Ledges sunset became a ritual. After three years of research, communities of passionate anglers, bikers, kayakers, surfers, rock climbers, brewers, and restaurateurs have been revealed to me. Within each of these communities there is a passion to protect, a pride of place, and an appreciation that inspires me every single day. The depth in which I now explore my home land is forever changed. I consider this book my sacred offering of unbounding gratitude to the communities and land of Northern Ohio.

A SHARED CLIMB

If you were to listen to RL Burnside's "Skinny Woman" and then listen to "Busted" by The Black Keys, you'd hear the inspirational influence Burnside's sound had on the Akron boys in the band, Dan Auerbach (guitar and vocals) and Patrick Carney (drums).

I was inspired by the outdoor books of Alastair Humphreys, Howler Bros, Yeti and Matt and Keegan Myers at M22. Heroic doses of inspiration flowed in from Yvon Chouinard, Kris McDivitt, and Rick Ridgeway of Patagonia. Not just their catalogs and books that I've been collecting since the 1970's, but the distinctive spirit of their Patagonia culture—a spirit humming deep in the stories, photos and art that show up in this book.

In 2018, as an adult beginner, I figured I'd free solo this book project. I calculated all I needed to write it was a thesaurus, William Zinsser's book *On Writing Well* and time. Then I'd take some more photos, lay it all out in Canva and self-publish it via the cloud-based platform I used for the first CVMA book, Susan's anniversary gift.

But then twenty-something Stefan Gaspar showed up in my life. Like the robin is a harbinger of spring, early collaborations with Stefan were harbingers of this book project becoming a village-making event.

I have no idea what Coop means by *these microadventures turn into macroadventures*. But should it all end with this Kickstarter campaign and the 220 books Jane the publisher prints, the aftermath of light will be that I was honored to have some beautiful people, teachers, and Ancestors show up to help.

Nate Padavick. While the stories got longer after Coop died, your initial 350-word guidance was gold. And because of you, I found Sarah Schmitz. Heidi Augustin, you helped me find my voice—and the confidence to let my *freak flag fly*. And you introduced me to my new hometown hero, John Debo, Jr. Judy Shaw—grateful we got to encourage one another as you wrote your second book ("Crooked River") and me my first. And you guided me to Jane Toma, the publisher at StreamlineCLE, and Kent-based artist David Wilson. David, I never got your mug shot to include on the *Contributors* page—but you belong there. Mighty Joe Graf—you know; LFG! Socrates, you and Coop know, too.

Sarah Kerr, for sharing your maps, indigenous wisdom and insights as I walk a path to honour and learn *grief* as a skill. Stefan for introducing old-head me to twenty-something AJ Sekerak. Julie (Jules) Robinson for pairing me up with Emily Cordonnier. Carol Turner for putting in a good word with your neighbors Derek and Janell DeYoung. Katie Coulton for Stephen Hannock—and sooo much more. From both sides of the veil, a mother and daughter—Mrs Burnham and Rachel Burnham Van Voorhis. Proud Sky, Robbie, Doc and Odie. You, The Backers, from near and far. Mike Hogan for re-acquainting me with Baroness Karen Christenze von Blixen-Finecke, which led to the "Buffalo Day" ritual.

Sarah Schmitz. Ha! We both thought it would be a one-and-done with a single illustrated map: "Gravel Bike the Mitchell's Ice Cream Loop"; so grateful it wasn't.

I still feel the *tingles* from September 10, 2023 at Solstice Steps—the day Emily, AJ, and I first met as a team, noshed on Martha On The Fly and felt the power and magic our confluence could have on this book. Free Range, you gathered the stories and photos, sensed the vibe and proceeded to paint a Masterpiece, bold and nuanced.

August 29, 2021, creek-walking Brandywine Creek to Brandywine Falls—the day you and I met, AJ. You became my flavorful belay partner on the shared climb to bring this book to life. I trust you with my life, pardner. Thank you for believing—for without you...

To Team Four: Susan, Cooper, Mackenzie, Michael, and Maxwell. And Team 5, born Saturday, May 7, 2022—the day Cooper became an Ancestor.

 It's been better together. Mitákuye Oyás'iŋ.

OTHER STUFF
Spotify: Jay Ungar's "Ashokan Farewell". Spotify: "Take a Little Walk" by Gregory Hoskins. YouTube: Mac Miller Performs "Ladders" with John Batiste & Stay Human on The Late Show with Stephen Colbert. Spotify: "We'll Meet Again" by Vera Lynn, Sailors, Soldiers & Airmen of Her Majesty's Forces, Roland Shaw and His Orchestra. Kris McDivitt Tompkins, Doug Tompkins and the *Wild Life* documentary, The Black Keys documentary *This is a Film About The Black Keys*. "Old Town San Diego Breakfast Tacos" at Michael Bruno's Blue Door Café.

↓ *Public art mural on the Boston Mills Road bridge pier created by Brazilian-born, United States-based Muralist Arlin Graff. Mural commissioned by Conservancy for CVNP to commemorate the 50th anniversary of Cuyahoga Valley National Park*

Meghan Winkler

↓ *Conservancy for CVNP, Cuyahoga Valley National Park and the Muralist, @arlin_graff*

CUYAHOGA VALLEY MICROADVENTURES